BAD YOGI

A Guidebook for the Rest of Us

Juliet,

To one of the most
inspiring, true and radiant
yoginis I've been graced
to know!

Greg Marzullo

ISBN: 1515176932
ISBN 13: 9781515176930

Om gam ganapataye namaha
I salute you Ganesh, spouse of the people, spouse of power and the remover of obstacles.

Om guruve namaha
I salute the guru, eternal teacher who shines light into darkness.

TABLE OF CONTENTS

INTRODUCTION

Put down the kale juice. Pick up a burger. Take a bite. Savor the cow meat. Hopefully, you put cheese on it, just for show. Let your canines do the work they were created for. Piercing. Tearing. After you've eaten the whole thing alongside some greasy fries, perhaps washed it down with a beer and even gotten laid afterwards, look in the mirror and say the following:

I am still a yogi.

Because you are. If you think being a vegetarian – or even better, a sanctimonious vegan – forswearing alcohol and extinguishing your sexual desire is the fast track to yogic heaven, you've failed. Your failure doesn't mean you *are* a failure, nor does it mean the very notion of failure isn't some human concept that keeps us bound in ignorance. As Krishna says in the *Bhagavad Gita,* "On this path, there is no failure."

But what do those words actually mean to modern yoga practitioners here in the west where we take up hobbies in order to conquer them, become self-appointed experts and then capitalize on them? There's got to be some failure! We're taught right and wrong in the postures, and after that, we're taught right and wrong in yoga's moral context. That's the progression most of us have experienced.

We join a yoga studio, start doing the asana and almost instantly we find that there's something more to the practice than sweating and touching our toes. We begin listening to a teacher who preaches what sounds like friendlier versions of the faiths we grew up with – be they Jewish, Christian or an agnosticism severely influenced by "traditional" beliefs. Don't harm others. Be compassionate. Stay present. Innocuous platitudes all.

We begin to change our life, or rather, we say that *yoga* has changed our life. We become more aware of what's going right in the world. After that wears off, we become more aware of what's going wrong in the world, or at least, yoga-approved topics of outrage: animal cruelty, environmental devastation, capitalism. We start to make conscious choices. No meat. More recycling. Stop judging.

Then, we really commit to the path. We haunt the studio, sometimes taking multiple classes a day. We carry around Patanjali's famed *Yoga Sutras*, and Sanskrit peppers our speech. We speak more softly, hand to heart, call people "brother" or "sister," and above all, we stay calm, collected, unruffled by the *citta vritti*, the whirling fluctuations of the mind, caused by our remaining attachments to an illusory notion of self.

And you know what you are?

A goddamned Puritan in black stretchy pants.

I get it. I loved my own tight yoga pants (especially the ones with the chakras down the leg), but eventually the artifice of doing yoga "right" – from the asana to its cognitive behavioral therapy brainwashing – became part of the problem in my life instead of part of the solution.

I came into the yoga scene with a sacred reverence for the body, sex, food and the totality of life, and early on in my teaching, I espoused an almost innate Tantric viewpoint, one where everything was sacred, from the outdoors to the outhouse. I'd studied with shamans and pagans for years before doing my yoga teacher training, and those wise teachers instilled in me the knowledge embraced by all earth religions: the manifest world is holy *just as it is*. It was easy to connect these beliefs with yoga asana, an embodied metaphor for the mysticism waiting beyond each Trikonasana, each inhalation and exhalation.

Maybe because I grew up in a crazy house where tacking with the changing winds of an unhinged parent was key to survival, maybe because I grew up gay and playing small was playing safe, or maybe it's something in my stars, but I've always been easily swayed by my surroundings. I want to please, to fit in, to be part of the group, and with spirituality and yoga, it was no different. Soon, the culture of the yoga world, from its genuine adherents to the vultures feeding on them, began to influence me.

I fell into the trap of the good kid, the earnest spiritual seeker who plays by the rules and does what the asana teachers and Indian gurus tell him to do. Be a vegetarian. Don't judge. Don't waste your *ojas*. Your desires are bad. Spend every moment chanting the name of God so you're not overwhelmed by petty thoughts. Anything you do for yourself shores up the tyrannical ego. Emotions have no eternal meaning and therefore have no meaning at all. There's a place out there that's better than this one – heaven is real! Everyone can be a *jivanmukta*, a person liberated from the bondage of this crap-ass world while still living.

I upped my meditation practice, replaced negative thoughts with positive ones just like Patanjali says and gradually replaced my love for the world with the disdain that had been lurking within me for years. Climbing over the walls of the enclosure is the only sane response to a life where everything is suffering.

During this time of intense practice, I knew I was really starting to progress along the path because my physical needs diminished. My interest in sex – always high – tanked, and my notorious love of food was replaced by boredom bordering on disgust. I was finally making some headway on this spiritual journey and the guidance of the gurus was dead-on. Because of my *sadhana*, my spiritual practice, even the body held no bondage for me. I didn't eat until mid-day and then only a little bit, just like the renunciates I'd read about in yogic texts. And I wasn't alone. Others in the yoga community were experiencing similar results. My yoga friends and I were on the same path of going the distance, reaching enlightenment, body be damned! We were the new ascetics, gaining great spiritual insight while chanting over our Vitamixes. I became more patient, more compassionate and less fiery tempered. I was downright *sattvic*, and people from students to friends to strangers in the street were responding in kind. They asked me ethical questions, sought me after class to tell me their stories, labeled me their pastor/rabbi/guru/guide, and they were almost scalping tickets for a spot in my classes.

There was only one small (very ironic) problem: I couldn't see. Multiple times a week, my entire field of vision was obscured by pulsating sunspots. It would strike randomly – while teaching, walking down the street, sitting on the metro – and would last anywhere from twenty minutes to an hour. Like an '80s song, I wore my sunglasses at night, because the bright lights of cars or streetlamps triggered the episodes. I couldn't look at my phone or computer until well past noon each day, and reading was a crapshoot.

After getting non-committal and unhelpful answers from all manner of western physicians, I finally spoke to my Ayurvedic doctor about it, who promptly asked about my eating habits. I told him that I wasn't really eating, partly because, by this time, I never felt hungry, and when I did eat, I was bloated, sluggish and slightly queasy. He said, "Your *agni* is shot. *Agni* is the body's fire, the fire of digestion – not only of food but of ideas and light. That's why you can't process/digest light, and you have these bouts of blindness." He put me on three meals a day, each one containing protein, and a rasher of herbs and spices.

On the new regimen, the trouble cleared up completely within two months. Yet to my surprise and chagrin, my saintly demeanor deteriorated with each breakfast, lunch and dinner. Impatience, a life-long challenge, jumped back into the ring, gloves raised and ready to kick ass after a long rest. Lust flared like a fire fed with dry wood, and no one was immune to the flames. Initially shocked, I soon had the sinking realization that I hadn't been more detached from the physical life during the past four years – I was just listless from hunger. There had been no spiritual advancement, only delusions of *jivamukta* grandeur. This entire episode showed me the dark side of my own escape fantasies and arrogance, neither of which was challenged by my yoga contemporaries but encouraged. The culture rewards the renunciate and patronizes the householder.

After my sight returned and I gained a few pounds, I began seeing the yoga world in a new light. I saw many students and teachers hawking the same wares I had offered, trying to live up to the image of a good yogi handed to them by books, gurus from India and their own asana teachers, all mixed with a hefty dose of American Puritanism. Everyone seemed to have the glassy-eyed, vacant look of a cult member, someone slipping off their sneakers and swilling down a Dixie cup of Kool-Aid at the end of all things. I heard teachers trot out the tropes that are part-and-parcel of the philosophy as starry-eyed students looked on and nodded their heads knowingly – yes, vegetarianism, yes, compassion, yes, ignore the wicked.

What I didn't hear was any mention of how to meet the darkness we carry within us – our grief, our rage, our betrayals, the lust for people and power, the capacity for breathtaking cruelty, an aching loneliness and the unending hope for a cease-fire in our own war-torn consciousness. There was talk about how to ignore the "negative" parts of who we are, but not what to do when ignoring them was no longer possible, when all that suppression finally failed and left us on the battlefield with no sword in the scabbard.

Perhaps more disturbing was that very few students were even asking about these topics, as if there was some tacit understanding that copping to their dark side was bad yoga. I heard the occasional brave student ask, "What do you do when it's just too hard to meditate, when you're depressed or dealing with too much?" All too often, pat answers were given, leaning again on ancient texts or so-called enlightened masters, but the question hung in the air like a fart in church.

All of these thoughts, recognitions and spiritual churnings came to a volcanic head on March 28, 2014. That morning, at thirty-seven years old, while sitting on the toilet, I had a stroke. I felt a numbness begin on the right side of my torso and spread past my ribs and down my leg. Ever the vain pragmatist, I thought, "They're not going to find me here," wiped my ass, flushed the toilet and crawled out of the bathroom. By that time, the numbness and paralysis seized the entire right half of my body, from shoulder to toe, as if I was split in two. After calling my husband and then the ambulance – not without some struggle, as the flat iPhone screen is a bitch to navigate if you're stroking out – I waited. Lying on the floor, I felt no fear. There was just stillness, like the silent expectation before a wave breaks and rolls to shore. Then, in a flurry, everyone arrived, I was strapped onto a gurney and raced to the hospital with sirens screaming and an oxygen tube looped over my ears.

An MRI revealed that I was, indeed, having a stroke – a thrombosis to the left thalamic region of the brain – and I was given a drug to flush all possible clotting from the body. The life-saving chemicals could also cause brain bleeding and death, so I was wheeled up to ICU where I had to remain absolutely horizontal for twenty-four hours. I spent long marches of time watching the clock, cruelly placed opposite the bed. My body begged for movement, for some escape from the increasing pain in my back, hips and shoulders, but no relief came. Only the waiting to see if the drug had done its work or if the stroke had spread like an oil slick suffocating a coral reef. How many species would be lost – sensations, cognitive thinking, motor control, word recall?

Sometime around dawn the next day, I heard the nurses whisper conspiratorially to one another in the hall. I only caught snatches of conversation, something about the guy next door, but in a few moments, their half-heard mutterings became terribly clear. They rolled my neighbor out of his room in a black body bag. It coasted past my window in an almost slow-motion crawl, a fluorescent-lit funeral cortege accompanied not by bagpipes or a twenty-one-gun salute but by the beeping and hissing of the machines that kept the rest of us from joining our fallen comrade.

The twenty-four hours finally passed, and the staff wheeled me back to the percussive MRI tube – its own near-death, tunnel-to-the-light experience after which the world has never felt quite the same. The images showed that the stroke had been stopped when the medication was administered the day before, and within a couple of hours, I teetered unsteadily down the hall alongside a physical therapist. (I absolutely credit the power of asana and muscle memory with getting me to walk so shortly after the stroke, although nothing has eased the remaining numbness in my body.)

Miraculously, the doctors sent me home that day, but as my husband rolled me out in a wheelchair, my thoughts turned to my unknown ICU neighbor, now dead. We weren't that different, he and I. Loved ones accompanied his exit, just as they did mine. The nurses bade him farewell as they did me. We both left on wheels, but he went out one end of the unit and I another. Yeah, life is short, precious and all that shit – everything I'd heard for years in spiritual circles – but now I *knew* it. Sooner than we think, a woman in scrubs will zip a glorified garbage bag over our face, and all the things that mattered won't.

In the months that followed, filled with unbelievable kindness and more casseroles than we could fit in our freezer, I went back to teaching, but increasingly, the yoga world felt like a farce, a mad theater of core-obsessed, surface-skimming, reductionist yoga fanatics, who made yoga a part of their daily regimen without making it a part of their life. When students brusquely pushed past others in a rush to leave the studio, or when they immediately disappeared into their phones after the final *Om,* or when they ignored people in the lobby to post status updates on Facebook (#sunsalute) or shoot Instagram pics of themselves doing an "advanced" pose, were they really diving into the murky hell that yoga asks us to visit? I felt increasingly panicked as I watched the carnival parade go by, fat adults buying cotton candy to silence their screaming offspring. There were days when I was shouting warnings in my head, and some days the inner voices became outer ones.

"Don't you see? You're all going to die before sundown! Enough with the masturbatory self-congratulating! Enough with the yogic passivity! Enough with the lies and the games and the hypnosis of happiness! Pull out your entrails and string them up for the world to see, shit and all. There is no enlightenment but this, the utter exposure of everything we hide away, the unmasking of all the monsters who are snarling and slithering inside us. *Moksha* is living without pretense, because when we do that, when we're implacably honest with ourselves, we're finally able to see God for what It is – a holy terror."

There's nothing nice about yoga at all, neither the asana practice nor the philosophy. There are no hearts and flowers, no puppy dogs, no sunshiny days perfect for picnics, and if there are, they're all just a set-up. Hearts explode, flowers wilt, dogs get hit by cars and ants overrun our basket of goodies. When we actually see – not casually look at – what yoga is offering us, what the stories and ancient texts are telling us again and again, we can move away from the infantile notions that keep us trapped in a childish life where God is good and playing by the rules gets us the prize.

It's high time we all grew up. Yoga in America has been in a preschool stage for decades; admittedly, it's an important stepping-stone, but if we're ever going to get into the rich soil of yoga – a down-and-dirty fully integrated yogic life – we're going to have to drop the sippy cup and take up the gin bottle. By anesthetizing yogic philosophy, knocking it off its Hindu bedrock and ignoring its rich mythical context, we've castrated a revolutionary path.

I've attended and (I'm ashamed to say) taught plenty of classes where meeting everyone's needs was the name of the game, where translating yogic belief into the Western vernacular was a way to make this foreign practice "accessible." Yet accessibility all too often turns into dumbing-down. Instead of shining a light into the dark corners of the soul, yoga teachers frequently enable students' addictions to validation and staggering narcissism. Yoga was not developed over thousands of years in the furnace of unblinking meditation, rigorous austerity and initiatory terror for us to live out our neurotic days as Stepford automatons; it's here to destroy us completely and leave nothing but a heap of ashes.

But that doesn't sell yoga mats.

This book is an attempt to redirect the yogic experience away from bumper-sticker pablum and root it back into the roiling stories and symbolism of India that teach us a great deal about the transcendent delights and abysmal degradations we face in a lifetime. There absolutely *are* answers to what ails us in a yoga practice, but they don't come from how we're currently doing it (or, darker still, how we're being taught it). While this book probably won't give you a yoga high, my hope is that it kicks you so far down the rabbit hole you won't know the highs from the lows, the good from the bad or the right from the wrong.

Now, *that's* yoga.

CHAPTER 1
DID YOU KNOW THERE'S A WAR GOING ON?

P ast all the down-dogging and warrior twos, a philosophy emerges in the yoga studio, often using the classical-era *Yoga Sutras* as the entry (and ending) point of an all-too-brief exploration of yogic teachings. After all, how much can a teacher really do in the first or last few minutes of a class besides read an inspirational quote or quip broadly about compassion? Patanjali's *Yoga Sutras*, a collection of intentionally short aphorisms about consciousness, are a perfect way to blend morality and time constraints, and if nothing else is mentioned from the *Sutras*, an American yogi will soon learn about the Shangri-la of yogic attainments: *ahimsa*, non-harming.

It seems like an easy thing to sign on for – don't hurt other people. No foul there. Fast on its heels comes the vegetarian proselytizing, sometimes subtle, sometimes abusive, and many of us buy into that, too. Truthfully, factory farming *is* a horror, so we nobly sacrifice that pork chop for a new code of ethics. Occasionally, we come across teachers who connect *ahimsa* to whatever war we're currently fighting or America's staggering racism. More likely than not, though, our pacific instructor is not mentioning these latter examples of *himsa* (harm) at all, choosing, instead, even at a studio owner's insistence, to steer well clear of tempestuous political waters. After all, let's not forget that yoga is for everyone, and we wouldn't want any student to feel uncomfortable or, worse still, upset. In an oversaturated yoga market, there are far too many studios that a consumer can choose instead of this one, so let's keep it all on the lighter side, okay?

This is all well and good for perpetuating an image of yoga as everyone's personal happy place where the lights are always bright and we're all getting skinnier, but what to do when conflict inevitably rises inside us? We're often torn in two by anger and even blinded by rage, but yoga frequently teaches us to ignore it and replace it with positive thinking. Yet that doesn't stop harmful thoughts and feelings from battering our peaceful demeanor on an almost daily basis.

The dark underbelly of *ahimsa* is that deep down we each carry a vicious capacity for violence. Ever watch children on the playground? There's always a roving pack of bullies preying on the weaker members of the herd. We can certainly pathologize those kids – they have the beginnings of such-and-such a disorder, or they must come from an abusive home, children don't come into the world like this – because that's an easier sell than the likelihood that some people (in fact many of us) harbor violent, terrible and ugly thoughts from an early age right to our deaths. With our back to the wall, we want to lash out physically or verbally. We want to punish others for their transgressions, and we get a high when we do. Nothing is as seductive as self-righteous anger, and taking out our frustrations on someone else feels downright sexy.

It's hard to match these dark urges with what we're hearing at the yoga studios (i.e. nonviolence is your ticket to heaven), so very often we bury them. We bury our rage, our cruelty and the almost animalistic need to dominate those around us. Your teachers are doing it, too. Down in the depths of who they are, their thoughts and feelings are just as bloody as yours. Pretending we're conscientious objectors to our own lust for battle just gives that fire more fuel. Better to fight than to burn.

≡⊱ ⊰≡

Arjuna gets the prize: Arjuna, one of the greatest heroes of India, was one of five royal brothers swindled out of their kingdom by a slimy rival cousin, Duryodhana. Forced to spend thirteen years in exile in the wilderness, along with the wife they all share (it's a long story), the brothers harbored thoughts of revenge against Duryodhana and his cronies. An epic war would eventually result from their bitter rivalry, and that battle would cause the death of millions. Knowing that a great fight was on the horizon, Arjuna journeyed deeper into the forest to worship Lord Shiva, one of the central gods of all Hinduism. The mortal hero needed Shiva's mightiest arrow, the *pashupataastra*, in order to win this war, so Arjuna stood on one leg for days, chanted mantras and damn near starved himself to death to get Shiva's attention.

High up on his mountain abode, Shiva had, indeed, noticed the warrior who prayed so fervently to him, and he decided to pay him a visit. First, though, he disguised himself as a forest-dwelling, rough-and-tumble hunter, and with a group of his devotees, also disguised as hunters, he set off to find Arjuna.

Chanting the holy *Om Namah Shivaya* mantra, Arjuna was meditating when Shiva's crew arrived. The hero's legs had long since gone completely numb from sitting in full lotus. His hair was a twisted nest of filthy braids, his beard had grown to his navel and his body was smeared with dirt and ashes from his sacrificial fire. Suddenly, a sound in the jungle jolted him from his meditative stupor – something crashed through the trees at a terrible speed! With a fighter's keen instinct, his eyes flew open, he notched an arrow in his legendary bow lying next to him and fired at the demonic boar hurtling towards him. Arjuna killed the beast in one shot, but once the creature dropped, sliding to a stop at his very feet, the hero discovered another arrow buried deep in its hide in the same spot as his own.

Arjuna untangled his legs, and as the blood painfully flowed back into them, a group of raggedy hunters emerged from the jungle.

"Not a bad shot," one of them said, "but our master nailed it first. The creature belongs to him."

"The hell it does," said Arjuna, his temper already rising. After all, he was a *kshatriya*, a man born for fighting, and no jungle trash could outshoot him.

"You're no match for our lord," the hunters scoffed. "Why is a meditating holy man shooting an animal, anyway? Shouldn't you be eating roots and praying to a god who doesn't listen?" They all started laughing, and Arjuna's entire body went rigid with anger. "Go back to your mantras. Leave the real work to real men."

With a roar, Arjuna demanded to see this so-called master of theirs, and in an instant, the crowd parted to reveal a large hunter who looked Arjuna up and down like a tiger eyeing a limping doe. The hunter grinned and shook his head dismissively, whereupon Arjuna yelled, "Fight me, you coward!" and lifted his bow. The pair began to duel while the crowd of jungle wanderers shouted epithets to distract Arjuna, but locked in complete concentration, his arrows still found their marks. The hunter did not bleed, however, but only smiled as Arjuna continued to shoot.

Then the unthinkable happened. After loosing an endless number of arrows, Arjuna ran out of ammunition.

"Impossible!" he cried. The gods themselves had given him that quiver, blessing it so that it would never be empty.

Not one to be deterred so easily, Arjuna ran at the hunter, planning to use the end of his bow as a lance and impale his enemy, but the jungle man quickly disarmed the young hero and flung the bow deep into the forest. Arjuna drew his sword and brought it down over the hunter's head, but the weapon shattered into a thousand pieces. Arjuna was almost frothing at the mouth by this point, and he started fighting the hunter hand-to-hand. They wrestled there amidst Shiva's devotees, and the god continued to smile, even laughing in delight as Arjuna punched, kicked and tried to break every bone in his body. Deciding enough was enough, the great god knocked out the wild warrior with a killer left hook.

Some time later, Arjuna woke. His head was throbbing, the mysterious hunter was gone, as was the wild boar, and Arjuna was left without weapons or hope. He sobbed there on the ground, realizing that he interrupted his great spiritual practice to get into a tussle with some lowly hunter, and now his hopes of getting the weapon in time for the upcoming battle had vanished. Completely devastated, he fashioned a Shiva *lingam* out of mud with his bloodied fingers, and after decking it with flowers plucked from the jungle trees, he prostrated before it and begged for forgiveness.

He looked up from the dirt and almost fainted again, this time from shock. The smiling hunter stood behind the lingam, and the flowers Arjuna had used for worship were woven through the wanderer's hair! Finally, the mortal realized that the hunter had been Shiva all along, and worse yet, Arjuna had fought him. He cried for mercy, but Shiva smiled more broadly still and said, "Arjuna, you are a *kshatriya*. You are meant to fight. You worshipped me the way you knew how to – with battle – and this was some of the best worship I've received in a very long time."

Shiva gave Arjuna the weapon he desired, and the hero returned to his brothers, knowing they were that much closer to winning the terrible war ahead.

Now, where the hell is *ahimsa* in all that?

Arjuna is not built to be a *brahmin*, a learned priest; that's
not his destiny. He was born into this world to fight. Should a
man gifted with the athletic ability for warfare sit on his ass all
day for years on end hymning god? Isn't that an actual betrayal
of what he was given by divine grace? Shiva didn't ask Arjuna to
be anything other than what he was; in fact, by engaging with
god through his own nature – that fiery-tempered, bloodthirsty,
determined nature – Arjuna was in a state of devotion.

When we're completely honest with who and what we are (as
opposed to what we think we should be) and we act from *that*
place, we are in communion with the divine. Everything else
fades to the background – all distractions inner and outer, all
neurotic concerns, all doubts – everything disappears and there
is only this blistering now-ness. Just you and Shiva, locked in
battle.

Current yoga culture is taking a bunch of *kshatriyas* (and artists and businesspeople and mechanics) and trying to turn them
into priests. Students are being told to overcome their nature,
because their nature is base and blinded by ignorance. Arjuna
was certainly blinded by ignorance, unaware of who stood in
front of him as he shot volley after volley at this seeming hunter,
yet he was rewarded for his efforts. This one story turns the
modern yoga world on its head. We're not going to find enlightenment or even peace by pretending to be what we're not.
In fact, ignoring the truth of who we are is a hindrance on the
path, because when baited in just the right way, we'll respond
exactly as Arjuna did.

Shiva will appear to each of us in different guises. He challenged
Arjuna to a battle of arms. He might seduce another into bed. He
could grace someone with artistic obsession or the gift for numbers.
Some will pore over ancient books in dead languages and others
will find peace raising and butchering animals. No matter the form,

our talents are the roads on which we travel to the Divine. These create our *dharma*, our purpose; our duty is to live it to the hilt.

Krishna says as much to Arjuna in the famous yogic text the *Bhagavad Gita*, which is a short interlude before a war orchestrated by Krishna himself. In yoga studios around the country, images of a flute-playing, flower-bedecked Krishna grace walls or altars. Practitioners can easily sidle up to a romantic cad who pets cows, dances with the ladies and steals butter. Most aren't told, however, that Krishna, an avatar of Vishnu, another of Hinduism's holy trinity, comes into the world to obliterate millions. One of his incarnation's main purposes is to incite and guarantee a war that wipes out an entire race of people, and him being God, you can be damned sure that's exactly what happens.

The *Mahabharata*, of which the *Bhagavad Gita* is a part, is India's greatest epic, and it chronicles the deadly war involving the five Pandava brothers and their treacherous cousins. Despite Krishna having sworn not to lift a finger in the actual fighting, the entire slaughter is laid at his feet like fruit on a mad deity's altar. The war is a great sacrifice, and during a famous moment of the *Bhagavad Gita*, Krishna reveals his true form to a terrified Arjuna who looks on as both armies rush into the flaming mouths of God. Who wouldn't rather worship the playful cowherd than this terrifying image? Yet the two cannot be separated. To split the lover from the fighter is a woeful misunderstanding of what the divine really is, and it leads us deep into the very ignorance we're trying to avoid with a myopic yogic rulebook bent on passivity and numbness.

At the pivotal moment right before the fight, Arjuna asks Krishna, who has agreed to be the hero's charioteer during the war, to take him out to survey the field. They draw up between the two armies, and were this a movie, the hero would now shout to the seemingly unflappable troops about honor and today being a good day to die. Once Arjuna looks at the enemy lines, however, his courage fails him; he's not afraid of fighting, so much as he's morally torn. His so-called enemies are members of his own family – his great uncle, his cousins, his archery guru, friends he's known his whole life long. The mighty Arjuna, the greatest archer on earth, without whom this war cannot be won, throws down his bow, sits on the battlefield and refuses to fight.

And what does God do? Does Krishna praise him for his wisdom? Does he say that, yes, indeed, killing is wrong and war isn't right? Not on your life. Krishna insults Arjuna's manhood and tells him to get his ass up and fight.

This is not to say the *Bhagavad Gita* lionizes war; everything was done to avoid it. During the brothers' thirteen years of exile, there were so many chances for the instigators to turn back, to show mercy to the wronged heroes, but the villains were having none of it. Before the armies took to the field, Krishna himself went to Duryodhana as the brothers' ambassador to ask for their half of the kingdom one more time. Duryodhana denied him and said, "I will not give them enough land to fit on the head of a pin."

We've all done that. We've all looked God in the face and said, "Not even enough land to fit on the head of a pin!" There are times in life when we've mired ourselves so deeply in stupidity that only a war will get us out. There's the terrible breakup that comes after ignoring the increasing signs of a deeply dysfunctional relationship. There's the time we end up in a screaming match with an employer because we didn't confront their mistreatment of us earlier. Perhaps we finally check in to rehab after we wake up in the hospital, or we begin to tend to our physical well-being only after a crippling illness that could have been avoided through preventative care. Refusing the emissary of truth always leads to war, and that war will have devastating casualties – our arrogance, pigheadedness, willful stupidity and all the other opiates we imbibe to inure ourselves to our darker secrets. No one wants to look down into the murky depths of their personality, yet, ironically, that's the only thing to heal us. It takes the courage of a warrior to set our sights on ourselves and shoot to kill.

Our whole life feels like a fight. One day after the next can seem like an endless slog just to make it to the day's end when the generals finally give the signal for a halt to the melée. There are moments every day when we want to give up – we're sick of work; we're tired of our partner; we can't bear the absolute stupidity of the people around us; we despair over the state of our neighborhood, city, country, world; we're broken by the craziness we carry inside of us and can't seem to escape no matter what philosophy we espouse. But despite all this, we're to get up and fight.

The warriors of the *Mahabharata*, like all warriors everywhere, battle on because it's better to die in the fray than live as a coward into old age. Krishna tells Arjuna that he'll be a laughingstock the world over and secure only infamy for himself if he doesn't rise up and do his duty. Much of the beautiful discourse of the *Gita* is about *dharma*, which often gets translated as duty. This concept is easily debased into a controlling precept used to imprison people in everything from sick relationships to socio-economic degradation. India's caste system – originally not an inherited curse, but a self-chosen path – is one example of *dharma* becoming a weapon. Abused women being told to stay in a violent household "for the children" is another misapprehension of duty. Whether we live in traditional India or modern America, we all struggle with the notion of duty (do your duty by your family, do your duty at your job), but this robs the word *dharma* of its richness.

I once heard Jyotishi and Ayurvedic practitioner Brendan Feeley define *dharma* as how we make meaning out of experience; it's not our duty, but our purpose. Beyond some externalized notion of duty, Arjuna's purpose is to fight and win this war. This is what he's meant to do with his life. All the years of training with weapons, untold hours of archery practice, meditation on military tactics and prayers to be the best bowman in the world have given him a legendary facility for battle. And now, when it comes to the moment at hand, he's going to walk away and deny the fulfillment of his purpose? Krishna tells him that it's better to struggle in his own *dharma* than to succeed in someone else's.

The trouble with how we're often being taught yoga is that we're not asked to examine what our *dharma* truly is; more likely, we're told what is *dharmic* (i.e. be good), but what is considered *dharmic* by some will be seen as *adharmic* (evil) by others. Who's to say what is the right course of action for any human being? We don't know what is right or wrong. We have agreements on behavior that help maintain a certain level of order, but we actually don't know what is ultimately good or bad in the universe. Good is usually defined by subjective criteria – whether or not it makes my life easier or happy – but what is good for me might be bad for you. We're all so addicted to feeling satiated and validated that we can't be trusted to understand what is good for ourselves, never mind anyone else. How many times have we hooked up with someone we know is a box of crazy just because that person was the only option, because they helped stave off the loneliness squatting in our empty apartment? The one-night stand helps keep the isolation at bay, but that doesn't help us to actually be rid of it altogether. What's good? Momentary satisfaction or long-term gain? A question put to us by Krishna in the *Gita*.

The struggle I hear most often from practitioners is how to be "yogic" and still get the job done, whether that job is in social work, litigation or pole dancing. For many students, there's a disconnect between high-flying yogic ideals and the fight on the ground. The confusion partly arises from an approach to yoga that keeps *dharma* in a gilded cage; it's pretty to look at but ultimately useless. We need tools about how to live a yogic life and defeat our competition in the courtroom, or fight the "enemy" or get more dollars stuffed down our panties. We can start by recognizing that the myriad activities we engage in are just the medium through which we make spiritual art of our lives. Whatever you're doing in the world of action could be your *dharma*.

Stop. Read that sentence again. Imagine for a moment that it's true. Imagine yourself free from moralizing, free from dualistic views on what's right about yourself and what's wrong about yourself. Imagine that whatever you did, from your job to meditation to the threesome you had on Saturday night, was a *dharmic* endeavor.

Because it is.

Krishna says to Arjuna, "All creatures are driven to action by their own nature ... Even the wise act within the limitations of their own nature. Every creature is subject to *prakriti*; what is the use of repression?*"

Prakriti is the manifest world, and it is holy. The sun, moon, stars. The rocks. The lightbulb over your head. Your clothes. Your skin, blood, cells. The forces of nature – atomic and subatomic. Gravity. Super String Theory. All of it is *prakriti*, and as Krishna teaches, we are all subject to it. We are in thrall to Mother Nature and our own nature. That being the case, what are we fussing about? We spend all this time in yoga fighting against our nature when even the wise succumb to the implacable tides of their idiosyncrasies. Some of us have the capacity to be great philosophers; others are brilliant soldiers or even criminal masterminds. *Prakriti* is the manifested quality of the Eternal Soul, and that Eternal Soul is the true meaning of the word "God," a poor, yet shorthand, translation of the Sanskrit *Brahman*. That God has no attributes, no personality, no rules, it doesn't care what you do or don't do – it is pure undifferentiated consciousness. *Prakriti* is God's power in action, and if all people are merely subject to *prakriti*, philosophers

---

* *The Bhagavad Gita*, trans. Eknath Easwaran (Berkeley, The Blue Mountain Center of Meditation, 1985).

and murderers alike, then all people are filled with God exactly as they are.

If you're a lover, be a lover. If you're a fighter, be a fighter. Whatever it is, go for broke. It's through our action, Krishna says, that we attain freedom.

The *Bhagavad Gita*, along with other yogic texts and stories, focuses on the elusive goal of *moksha*, liberation. I'll tell you straight up I have no idea what that is, and, for some, my ignorance is reason enough to put this book down and go find someone who is signed-sealed-and-delivered enlightened. I wouldn't blame you.

Do me a favor, though. Once you've found the guru and gained the wisdom, tell me the good news not from the mountaintop, but after you've come back down and actually kept your yogic cool while slogging it out in the trenches. To me, enlightenment isn't the great escape (although that would be lovely); it's deep engagement. We don't reach higher states of consciousness because we put down our arrows and refuse to fight the enemy. We gain wisdom by crawling on our belly through shit, piss and blood. When we cry and rage and stop believing in God (because what kind of divine power would put us through this hell?), then we've done the work. Be an atheist because God betrayed you, and you'll really find liberation. I'm not sure what enlightenment looks like, but I suspect we'll be covered with scars when we get there.

After the *Bhagavad Gita* comes to a close and Arjuna's fears are allayed, the action resumes, like a movie coming out of freeze frame, and although Arjuna has returned to his ass-kicking heroic self, he still suffers occasional doubt. All the pretty words he just heard are about to be put to the most awful of tests. When Arjuna confronts his beloved great-uncle, the mighty warrior Bheeshma, on the battlefield, he can't quite bring himself to kill him. He holds back from his very best, and twice during these encounters, Krishna gets so angry that he jumps down from the chariot and does a kind of Vishnu Incredible Hulk routine. He gets bigger, the skies go dark, his skin burns a fiercer shade of blue and he stalks across the field, ready to kill Bheeshma, who falls to the ground in ecstasy, overjoyed to receive death at the hands of God. Arjuna leaps in front of his great friend and charioteer, begging Krishna not to go back on his word and to stay out of the fight. If God Himself were to break his vow, the planets would cease to hold their orbits, he cries. Krishna relents and Arjuna fights more ferociously than ever, eventually having a definitive role in Bheeshma's demise.

What happens when something or someone dear to us blocks the path of our *dharma*? The story tells us that the obstacle *will* be overcome, one way or another. Arjuna or Krishna will kill Bheeshma, but either way the old man is going down. After the lessons of the *Gita*, Arjuna knows that the war will unfold and that millions will die. He can resist, he can cry about it, he can run off the battlefield screaming, but ignoring a problem won't make it go away. We can't un-know something we've learned about ourselves, others or a difficult situation. Truth will out.

Sanskrit is India's sacred language, not spoken on the street but used exclusively for rituals and in sacred texts like the *Gita*. Some scholars consider it the spiritual language *par excellence* because of its innumerable connotative meanings that lead one into a labyrinth of meditative self-inquiry. In Sanskrit, the word *satya* translates as truth. Its root word, *sat*, also means "being," so truth is linked to being, to our very existence. Likewise, the word *asatya* means untruth, but there's a hitch to its second meaning of "not being": it's impossible. We live in a manifested world with physical properties. Everything in the universe is being, is existing. Gandhi went a step further with the connection between untruth and non-being, saying that since there can't be "not being," then ultimately there can't be untruth. Martin Luther King, Jr. reflected this idea when he said, "the arc of the moral universe is long, but it bends towards justice." Sooner or later truth must win the day, because untruth isn't real. Whatever is untruthful in our lives will eventually fade and die.

We all know what it is to live in untruth. Lovers remain in painfully acrimonious partnerships long past the sell-by date, yet they make no move towards ending it until it blows up in some spectacular fashion. We've all met (or been) someone in their middle years who is so embittered by not risking more to follow their dreams that their every moment is steeped in regret and criticism of others. Jobs we hate. Choices we know are sapping us of peace. We are beset by *asatya*, and there we stand, bows in hand looking across the field of *dharma*. In order to become fully conscious, to live without excuses or regrets, there are times when we have to notch the arrow and kill the thing that's killing us.

Of course, this is all metaphorical talk, but the heaviness of snuffing out a familiar way of life feels as epic as Arjuna shooting his great uncle full of one hundred arrows. We must destroy to move forward. If something is in your way, in the way of you living your purpose, blow it up. Our only act of free will is to pull the trigger before God does it for us.

Once we've done it, followed our *dharma* despite personal risk, we wait, expectantly, for the prize. This is how we've been taught everything from catechism to corporate ladder climbing: work hard, do your job (read: duty) and you get what you deserve. But that's not really true, is it? Some people do everything by the rules and they get the shaft. Some people play dirty and they pull a lump of gold out of the pile of shit.

During the *Mahabharata* war that claims the lives of millions, down to almost the last man, Arjuna is not unscathed by tragedy or protected from loss because he's living the dream. His own son, a shining warrior, is killed by treachery after putting up a daring fight against the enemy. Arjuna is away from that part of the battlefield, lured into a fight elsewhere, and when he returns to camp, he's completely shattered by the news. His duty, his purpose, his *dharma* led him to this exact moment of undoing. There was no other way this was going to go. He's a warrior. His son was a warrior, and despite their prowess, there was a good chance that they would die in battle. This should come as no surprise, yet of course, it does. We're always blindsided by our own frailty and by the irrefutable fact that following our path doesn't always feel good. That's because it's not meant to.

Life is a battlefield, and despite our greatest efforts, all our training and skill, we're not walking off the same way we walked on. There will be spatters of blood, scars, gore, even missing limbs. Pieces of us will get cut away when we move too slowly or don't see the arc of the enemy's battle axe, and we will be hewn down to nothing. And God presides over this mighty bloodletting that is our life. Everything that we do in every single moment of this incarnation is a slaughter. Some of it seems absolutely sweet and kind (falling in love, a promotion, rare moments of peace and beauty), but they're all a setup for the demise, for the stripping away of those same fleeting victories. Krishna oversees the sacrifice that is our heartbreak, grief and rage, just as he witnesses Arjuna's oath that he will either kill his son's murderer the next day or kill himself by sunset.

We don't fulfill our purpose in order to win the lottery. We fulfill our purpose because we're driven to it. The world's artists stand as perfect testament to this. Ask any actor, violinist, dancer, painter or writer why they do what they do in the face of insurmountable odds, and you'll hear them speak of being possessed by the spirit of their art. Catching the Muse isn't just Victorian poetry; more often, the Muse catches the artist and chokes the life out of them until they do the work. Does this grant fame, fortune or even the ability to pay one's bills? Fat chance. What it does guarantee is a life filled with meaning – not "success," but a point to the whole charade.

Most people are artists in their own sphere of life – be it business or poetry – but because many ignore the call to their purpose, we have a culture filled with pale drones languishing at computer terminals under fluorescent lighting. Sure, it might be a "safe" life, far from the battlefield where the risk is tremendous, but it's also a numb life. Yoga does not ask us to be numb to experience. In fact, as Krishna does in the *Gita*, it demands that we scream as we run across blood-stained grass, whirling a sword over our head and rejoicing that we're given a chance to slay the only thing worth killing: our ignorance.

When it's all over and an entire race of people has died, the five brothers return to an empty kingdom, filled only with widows and old men. They atone for the lives they destroyed through the appropriate rituals, because even after that God-sanctioned slaughter, there's cleansing that needs to be done. Eventually, the kingdom is set aright and it enjoys years and years of blessings and plenty. Peace comes only after great strife. There cannot be contentedness without long periods of agonizing yearning. As Krishna says in Arjuna's fateful moment of crisis, nothing easily gained is worth having. The struggle for wisdom and a connection to God is not to be won without a fight, so if we want peace, it's time we all saddle up and prepare for war.

CHAPTER 2
A GOD BETWEEN THE SHEETS

We discover all sorts of terrible things while roaming the battlefield, many of which we'd rather ignore completely. Our yoga teachers encourage us to look the other way when confronted by "negative" emotions and thoughts – change your focus, change your mind – but is that actually working for anyone? No one can just think their way into long-lasting joy. Inevitably, we find ourselves in the grip of wild thoughts, emotions and desire, the *bête noire* of yogis everywhere. Nothing causes more of a ruckus in our lives than desire, and sexual desire is cast as the mustache-twirling villain in an otherwise pure life. Sacred texts and wise teachers from India espouse the virtues of *brahmacharya*, often translated as "celibacy" or sometimes pitched to a reluctant public as "continence." If we just move beyond sex, we'll all have unlimited stores of energy, be more peaceful – hell, we'll even stay younger longer! Sit. Meditate. Think of God. Sex only wastes your time, gets you in trouble.

And you know what? They're right. Trying to get some ass is a lot of work. From endless hours at a gym, to dieting, blow-outs, makeup, the right clothes, mind-numbing bar talk (or, worse: mind-killing app chat), everyone has become attached to the hunt.

Entire identities are wrapped around our sexual availability, prowess and scorecard, furthered by social networking sites that reduce interpersonal interactions to pie charts. Don't forget the awkward morning-afters or explanations that the sex is great but you don't like them as a person. Even when married, the sticky web of desire is still at play with flirtations and affairs consuming more time than usual because of the duplicity needed to keep it all hush-hush.

Perhaps, as the sages say, it *is* better to avoid the sex problem altogether and just get over it – but it isn't that easy. Celibacy hasn't worked for countless Western monks, and it's not working for countless Eastern ones, either. Most people just aren't ready for it, and avoiding our sexuality through a spurious practice of celibacy only causes the desire itself to gain power. No use pretending to be Mother Teresa when you're more the Marquis de Sade.

American yogis love to enshrine people we view as the real deal – a wise teacher who, to all appearances, is a font of yogic inspiration and lives the path of speaking compassionately, eating those *sattvic* meals of mung beans cooked without salt and transcending all dirty, icky sexual impulses. Those sainted beings have realized, as some yogic texts say, that the body is nothing but a bag of blood, pus and bile, and honestly, who wants to rub two of those together? Except at some point, that same wise teacher is found in the midst of a drunken orgy with a bunch of students. That's when we all turn on the guru, crying that we've been betrayed – we *believed* in them and they lied to us. How could they do this and fall so far off the path of righteousness? Better to ask why we, as Western practitioners, are so invested in a teacher's perfection.

We *want* to believe that someone can move beyond the degradations of the human experience, because we fervently hope that we'll be able to do the same. We know there's something wrong with us, something hopelessly ignorant (other faiths call it "original sin"), and we need a good person to save us. Jesus isn't around, but Sri Sri Yoga-ji is! Yogis across the country are being told by supposed gurus to go beyond our impulses, to ignore our root humanity, and we lap it up like kittens drinking poisoned milk. The horrible, nasty, heartbreaking, unspoken truth about our desires is that we won't get over them until we've fulfilled all of them. Only boredom from overuse frees you from desire.

⇒╫⇐

Let's make a deal: On the banks of a jungle river lived a fisherman and his daughter Matsyagandha, so named because she stank of fish. (Being pulled from the belly of a fish as an infant will do that, but that's another story). One day the great sage Parasara came to the fisherman's hut and demanded to be rowed across the river. As the fisherman was busy, he had his daughter head to the boat to row the old man to the other side. After just one look at her, Parasara was so completely inflamed by the girl that he wanted her then and there.

Now, Parasara was no newbie to the spiritual life. This wasn't some lusty teenager who took the vow of *brahmacharya* one week ago. Parasara was a *maharishi*, a great seer. He composed some of the original hymns of India's holiest and oldest spiritual text, the *Rig Veda*, along with a compilation of sacred stories of Vishnu and the foundational treatise on the cosmos and Hindu astrology. This guy was a big deal, and still, he was awash with desire for the young Matsyagandha.

As she rowed him across the water, the old man grabbed her hand and expressed his longing for her. She tried to rebuff him gently, reminding him of his exalted status and her lowliness. Still, he would not be denied, and she, being concerned he'd sink the boat in his ardor, convinced him to wait until she got to the other shore. Once they landed, he again caught her hand, and again, she hesitated, reminding him that her father could see them from the other side. With his magical powers, Parasara shrouded them in a dense fog. He clasped her closely to him and even changed her fishy reek to the irresistible scent of jasmine that wafted from her for leagues around them. She hesitated once more, saying she'd likely become pregnant by the *rishi's* powerful seed and then she'd be ruined. In his lust for her, he hurriedly told her that she could have whatever she asked for if she lay with him.

"I want to always smell like I do now. I want a son who will be a great *rishi* like you, and I want my virginity to be restored so that I won't be shamed in the village."

"Done!" cried the sage, adding, "And I'll bless you further: Your son will be one of the most famous poets of all time, renowned throughout the universe for his words and his wisdom!"

With his promises ringing in her head, Matsyagandha took the old man into her arms. After he spent himself inside her, he bowed to her, the young girl who had unexpectedly kindled the flames of desire in a mighty *rishi*, and then he vanished into the mist. Sure enough, she was pregnant instantly, and just as magically, she gave birth to a full-grown *rishi* right there on the riverbank. His skin was dark, he was wise beyond all telling, and true to Parasara's word, this son of a sage and a fisher girl became a legendary poet, organizing the Vedas and composing the great *Mahabharata*. He even became the grandfather of the five Pandava brothers themselves!

Parasara wasn't ruined by his time with Matsyagandha. He didn't become a gravedigger or lose all his knowledge. He carried on with his life of devotion, perhaps even a bit wiser for having had the encounter, because he engaged with the desire itself. We demonize desire, because it's been demonized for us. Lust is bad. Sex gets us in trouble. Longing only ends in grief. In actuality, nothing is bad. Nothing is good, either. Sex is sex. Lust is lust. Desire is desire. It surges through our body like an uncontrollable fire and threatens to burn us up if it's not fed. No one can avoid it, because it's a part of being here in this world. If someone like Parasara, full of wisdom, having performed rigorous spiritual austerities like fasting and praying for years on end is swayed by a young girl's beauty, what's to become of the rest of us?

Sexuality is one of the essential metaphors of our existence. Everything in our lives can be viewed as a coming together of disparate parts into a unified whole. "Yoga means union" is a popular saying in the yoga studio, but we've sapped the sensual meaning from the union. Union of what? What does union even mean? Bringing two into one. What is sex? Bringing two into one. Two bodies are literally joined and explode in an ecstatic release of power and fluids that create union. This is what we are supposed to be doing with the divine. Coming into union with God is not a church pancake supper, but nothing short of a sheet-shredding orgasmic love fest.

Bhakti yoga, the yoga of love and devotion, acknowledges our longings and connects them directly to God. Those devoted to this path use desire as an engine to propel them straight into a relationship with the divine, some male devotees going so far as to dress up in drag as Krishna's erotic consort Radha. They're trying to get his attention, trying to lure the great lover into their arms and hearts, so they can be forever in his ecstatic embrace. They know his stories, and they know how Radha and Krishna can't live without each other.

⚊⁖⚊

Holy hanky-panky: From infancy, Krishna lives with a tribe of cow herders, good people who love and care for the charming blue boy. As he grows into a handsome young man, though, the women of the village are seized by a love different from motherly affection; they turn randy, indeed, and the god does nothing to dissuade them. In fact, late at night, the blue one plays his flute in the forest and the village women go running through the trees to meet him, leaving behind their husbands and families for a chance to be wrapped in the dark arms of Krishna. There, in the jungle, they dance the famed *Rasa Lila*, often pictured in art as a circular dance of women with a Krishna for each one of them. Being God, he gets to have it all and show each one a good time, but there is one woman who takes pride of place: Radha.

Radha is no simple village girl; she's the Goddess Herself, the Divine Feminine made human in order to meet Krishna in the mortal world. Whenever she's not with him, she pines for Krishna, yearns to be by his side, goes mad from desire for him, but she's also wildly jealous when she discovers him making moves on any other woman. In her anger, she withdraws from him, showing him that he can't treat her like some common floozy. Krishna, the god of all the worlds, is absolutely crushed and filled with a fiery longing for his Radha, until finally, she overcomes her wounded pride, joins him in the forest and rides him until they're both lost in the climax of love.

When the story of Krishna and the *Rasa Lila* is told by modern gurus, they're quick to point out that this is all metaphor. It's not about sex at all (mustn't let the groundlings think there's anything sacred about this whole desire thing), and while they're right in that the story is metaphor, they're wrong to think the metaphor itself is somehow beneath God. Eleventh-century Indian poet Jayadeva wrote the *Gitagovinda*, a series of verses about the love drama between Krishna and Radha, and in true poetic fashion, he doesn't shy away from the sensuality of the story.

After Radha spurns Krishna, she is tormented by longing and fantasizes about the god ravishing her:

> *I fall on the bed of tender ferns; he lies on my breasts forever.*
> *I embrace him, kiss him, he clings to me drinking my lips …*
> *My eyes close languidly as I feel the flesh quiver on his cheek.*

My body is moist with sweat; he is shaking from the wine of lust…
My hair is a tangle of wilted flowers; my breasts bear his nail marks.

Krishna, too, is forever dreaming of the beautiful Radha:

Your heavy black sinuous braid
May perversely whip me to death.
Your luscious red berry lips, frail Radha,
May spread a strange delirium.
But how do breasts in perfect circles
Play havoc with my life?

Finally, after a torturous back and forth, they meet again and Krishna begs her for her love, the man begs the woman to release him from his maddening desire, God begs the devotee to love him, which she does beyond his wildest dreams:

Displaying her passion
In love play as the battle began,
She launched a bold offensive
And triumphed over her lover.
Her hips were still,
Her vine-like arm was slack,
Her chest was heaving,
Her eyes were closed.
Why does a mood of manly force
Succeed for women in love?

After his epic orgasm, she tells him to adorn her:

'My beautiful loins are a deep cavern to take the thrusts of love –
Cover them with jeweled girdles, cloths, and ornaments, Krishna …

Paint a leaf on my breasts!
Put color on my cheeks!
Lay a girdle on my hips!
Twine my heavy braid with flowers!
Fix rows of bangles on my hands
And jeweled anklets on my feet!'
Her yellow-robed lover
Did what Radha said.

There's nothing unclear about Jayadeva's words, which forego suppressed, philosophical expositions of the Godhead in favor of erotica. As a result, we not only have a work of art that makes our pulse race, we're graced with a true understanding of what a relationship with God is like: a hot night of lovemaking.

Jayadeva also reveals an unexpected turn between us and God, between Radha and Krishna: the divine *wants* to be with her. This isn't the unworthy devotee groveling at the feet of the deity, like a codependent lover begging some lout to take her back. Krishna wants her just as much as she wants him. Much of our spiritual upbringing paints the worshipper as a bad child trying to regain God's favor, but here we, like Radha, are riding God to orgasm because he desires us with the same ferocity that we do him.

All of this is explained through the symbol of sexual play, and without having gone through it ourselves, how are we truly to understand this kind of relationship with the divine? We can't know what lovemaking is like by reading about it; likewise, we can't know an intimate relationship with God without experiencing it on every level of our being. The ancient storytellers and poets use this sacred sex story to teach us of God because they know it's a key into our awakening. Everyone in the world goes through the pangs of desire for another person – the obsessive thinking about them, the

---

* Jayadeva, *Love Song of the Dark Lord: Jayadeva's Gitagovinda*, ed. and trans. Barbara Stoler Miller (New York: Columbia University Press, 1977).

fantasizing about their body, their eyes, their hair, what you would do with them if they were in your hands, perhaps even pleasuring yourself with their picture in your mind. None of this is abnormal, and neither is any of it ungodly. You have desires. Embrace them.

In Paramahansa Yogananda's seminal work *Autobiography of a Yogi*, he describes an encounter between his family's guru Lahiri Mahasya and the fully realized avatar Babaji, a magical sage who lives in the Himalayas, praying and teaching an elite group of disciples. One night in the wilderness, while in the great avatar's retinue, Lahiri comes upon an enchanted golden palace, brightly lit and filled with revelry. He turns confusedly to another of the disciples who ushers him into the party, telling him that Babaji conjured up this palace for Lahiri, because it was Lahiri's one remaining desire. Once Lahiri parties for the night in this palace, he's done with his attachments to the world and will attain *moksha*. Lahiri could not reach enlightenment until he'd achieved every single one of his desires. Everyone has to do everything because only when we've had our fill can we let go of the longing.

Lahiri's dream for a palace party is one thing; the cravings that threaten to destroy us or ruin others are where this all gets complicated. Addicts will use until they've had their fill or die. They have to hit bottom before they start the long climb out of the abyss, and it's the same with all of us, classic addicts or the everyday addicts who are slaves to their mental habits instead of a drink. There are longings down in our consciousness that are begging to be let out, be they sexual, destructive or just plain cruel, and we can actually release the pressure valve by being absolutely honest with who we are. ("Hello, my name is Marjorie, and I'm [petty, cruel, a liar, lustful, arrogant, vindictive, etc.]") On the yogic path, we're taught that these naughty desires are part of the "false self," some compartmentalized portion of our personality that isn't really based in any reality so we don't have to pay it any mind. Until you're unflinchingly truthful about who you are, though, that desire is going to eat you alive. In fact, through the terrible grace of God, you'll be put into a situation where you're forced to confront the darkest desires you have.

Why are so many people in public office, or in positions of so-called moral authority, literally caught with their pants down? How many homophobic and sex-phobic pastors or politicians are revealed to be trolling for sex in bathrooms or hiring prostitutes? Think of all the Wall Street barons laid waste when their bottomless penchant for greed comes to the light of day or the sports stars whose lust for winning leads to doping. The number is high enough to warrant an examination not of the desire itself, but of the attempt to suppress it. The stifling of desires is nothing but a lie, and lies, eventually, become untenable.

We begin by weaving a story antithetical to what our actual nature is (I'm above this, God says this is bad, that's not really who I am), and sooner or later, a whole new identity gets created out of the smoke-and-mirror game we've played. We start slicing ourselves into little pieces – this is the me who volunteers at the shelter, this is the me who goes to yoga seven days a week, this is the me who works hard at the office, this is the me who plays wiffle ball with the neighbor kids, and then there's this other person who watches prison porn to get off before bed every night. We've all got our prison porn and the sooner we own up to it, even embrace it as a vehicle to becoming conscious, the further we get on the spiritual path.

The great 20th-century Kaishmir Shaivite teacher Swami Lakshmanjoo said, "Impurity isn't dirt. Impurity is ignorance." The only ignorance we harbor is the mad belief that one thing is holy and another is not. Buying into this lie immediately creates duality, a me-versus-the-world attitude that ruins us. Getting lost in an Internet porn loop isn't the problem. Pretending we're above it, saying it's wrong, feeling guilty afterwards, making promises we'll never do it again, shaking our head derisively when someone else gets caught doing it at work – that's the problem. Dirt is dirt. Nothing more or less. As yogis, our goal is to see the dirt, smell it, taste it even, as divine. It's all well and good to know God is present when we're looking at a blooming rose or a spectacular sunrise – it's enlightenment to know the same when we're scraping dog shit off our shoe. The only way to do that is to go to the dog park looking for steaming heaps of excrement. We can't find God in anything if we've shut ourselves off from everything.

⇌

The hooker with a heart of gold: Once there was a family of prostitutes, and among them lived one named Mahananda. She was stunningly beautiful, did really well for herself and was a great Shiva *bhakta*, a devotee of Shiva. Doing everything in his name – from cooking dinner for her family to servicing the endless number of men she took to her boudoir – she had eyes only for Him. She even kept a little pet rooster and monkey that she dressed in jewelry dedicated to the god. She did it all for Shiva and never was confused about the seeming paradox of worshipping God while having sex with strangers for money.

One day a trader arrived at her door, and upon seeing his sacred jewelry, ash-smeared body and dread-locked hair, Mahananda instantly recognized him as a fellow Shiva *bhakta* and graciously ushered him into her home. She fed him while they talked and laughed together, and during their lunch, she couldn't help but notice the beautiful, jewel-encrusted bracelet on his wrist.

"How much for the bracelet, my friend?" Mahananda asked.

"How much do you think it's worth?" he said, slyly.

"I, Mahananda, the harlot, will marry you for three days and nights in return for that bangle."

"Swear by the sun and the moon, say *satyam*, truth, three times and touch my heart," said the merchant excitedly, "and we'll be wed!"

Mahananda did as he said – what's three measly days, after all – and the whore had a husband. After she took her oath, he showed her a beautiful crystal *lingam* that he always carried with him.

"This is as important to me as my very life," he said devotedly. "Now that we're married, I leave it with you for safekeeping." As a fervid Shiva *bhakta* herself, she understood the great trust he was placing in her, so she locked the lingam away in a secret place in the house.

With the formalities done, they got down to business in the bedroom. They went at it all night, and he demonstrated a level of skill she'd never experienced before. Usually, the men who came to her were there for their own pleasure, but this one got off on driving her wild with orgasmic delight. They were a perfect match for each other, both skilled artists of lovemaking, and after hours of worshipping one another, they fell into a deep and well-earned sleep.

In the hour before dawn, they awoke to the screaming of her pet rooster and monkey. The couple stumbled out of bed and into the main room of the house, where they were jolted awake by an awful sight. Black smoke billowed from every doorway, tongues of fire licked at the walls and the roof was close to bursting in a terrible conflagration. Quickly Mahananda swept up her pets and tossed them out of a nearby window in the hopes of rescuing them, and then the newlyweds fled. The neighbors ran to the inferno, trying to put out the fire with buckets, pitchers, even cups of water, anything they could find, but by the time the sun crested the horizon, the house was nothing but a smoking ruin.

Both Mahananda and her husband stared at the ashes, and he said grimly, "There's one more fire to set before this day is done."

She looked at him confusedly.

"My crystal lingam is destroyed, and so am I. Build a pyre, wife. I, too, am going to the flame."

Stunned, she did as he asked, hiring local men to build a massive funeral pyre for this man she hardly knew but felt strangely connected to. When everything was ready, her husband climbed onto the timbers, sat in a full lotus posture and began chanting a mantra to Shiva. The townsmen put their torches to the wood, and it went up in a flash, carrying the still-meditating trader off to the next world.

With the light of the fire dancing madly across her face, Mahananda decided that she, too, would walk into the flames. Her friends and relatives tried to talk sense into her, but she felt so guilty for the man's death and so devoted to him after only one night together that there was nothing left in this world for her. She walked toward the burning pyre, chanting the same mantra her husband had used, and just as the fire reached for her, a man – no, a god! – emerged from the blaze.

Shiva himself was standing between his singular devotee and her doom. He had disguised himself as the traveling merchant to visit Mahananda, and he was absolutely enthralled with her.

"Your worship of me has been exquisite your whole life long," said the god of gods in a rumbling voice. "Ask for any boon, and it shall be yours."

"*Mahadev*, great God, please allow me and my entire family to serve you and never be parted from you again. Let us be free from this world forever."

Shiva granted her wish and spirited Mahananda and her people off to his blessed kingdom where they lived in his presence. He even blessed Mahananda's beloved rooster and monkey, leading them to *moksha* in their next lives.

We moralize, thinking we understand God's mind, but we don't. We believe that living up to the expectations of a regimented system or a religious authority, be it Western or Eastern, earns us a spot in heaven, but the only real path to follow is that of totally loving God. The heroine of our story understood that there is no delineation between "sacred" and "profane," that all work and action done in God's name is instantly sanctified because all things are God. She didn't compartmentalize her job from her worship, nor did she think that her work as a prostitute somehow disqualified her from a holy life. Giving some greasy, hard-up husband a blowjob for money can be as honorable a ritual as chanting prayers over a fire. There is no difference except for that created by our faulty perception, and this disparity – sacred vs. profane –is the only *Maya* (illusion) that exists.

Modern yogis love to toss around the word *Maya*, labeling experiences, choices and even people with the term, and nothing gets called *Maya* more frequently than our desires. Yet *Maya*, often personified as a goddess, is the clearest mirror into our soul. Every moment of every day, through our experiences in the world, She tries to show us the truth of things – nothing lives forever, people are liars, *we're* liars, joy is as temporary as sorrow, good and evil are relative –but still, we aggressively persist in pretending none of this is true.

Maya is perhaps the greatest guru of them all, endlessly patient, applying the pressure more and more until we cave and beg for mercy. The world is our teacher. Life, with all of its staggering beauty and torment, is our teacher. Gurus often say the world is an illusion, and while it's true that nothing in the world is permanent, that doesn't make it illusory. Our mistake is attributing long-lasting meaning to the fleeting experiences of a lifetime. We plant the flag of our personality on the beach of a job, a relationship, even a childhood trauma and spend the rest of our lives flailing away at the tides eroding the ground below us. We think we know what we're about, until *Maya* throws us for a loop with an unexpected turn of fate – love where we weren't looking for it, financial disaster, a narrow escape from death – and we learn a terrifying truth: She owns our ass. We are not in control of our fate any more than the family dog is. It might tug against the leash and hold it in its mouth, but ultimately, there's still a collar around its neck.

⇌⇋

Now that's a pedicure: Once the three great gods Brahma, Vishnu and Shiva, known as the Creator, the Preserver and the Destroyer, respectively, were granted an audience with the supreme Goddess. It was during the time when only a vast, undifferentiated ocean existed in the cosmos. There was no earth, no realm in which the three could do their *dharmas*, and the trio was somewhat despondent about not having a playground for their power. From afar, the Goddess saw their confusion and decided to show them the true nature of existence.

She spirited them away in a magical flying machine, and along their travels they stared in wonder as a version of the earth emerged from the vast darkness of the cosmos. It was the planet they had hoped to create, but they saw it come to life in a location far away from their own corner of space. Surrounding this doppelgänger earth were all the realms of heaven and the nether worlds that Brahma, Vishnu and Shiva had talked about crafting back home. Things got stranger still when they saw other versions of themselves in this alternate universe. Brahma watched another version of Brahma creating, while sitting atop a lotus flower. Shiva watched another Shiva meditating in a cave on a mountain. Vishnu discovered another Vishnu in a heavenly realm lying next to a heavenly Lakshmi fanning him and shooting him amorous looks. All three of the gods then stared at each other, bewildered by what they were seeing.

"Who am I?" they all wondered.

The flying contraption whisked them away to a higher realm where the gods of wind, water, fire, death and other primordial powers lived in their own eternal city. Further and further, the craft flew until at last they came to the seat of the Goddess, and it was Vishnu who recognized her.

"It's the Devi Bhagavati!" he cried in bliss. "Mahavidya Mahamaya! The Great Goddess, She who is the supreme knowledge and the supreme illusion!"

Brahma, Vishnu and Shiva stumbled out of their ship, almost blinded by her radiant beauty, and as they approached the Goddess, seated on a mighty throne, they were magically transformed into women. Overcome with rapture, they threw themselves down into a full prostration before the Great Mother, and when they raised their heads ever so slightly to catch a glimpse of her blessed feet, they became transfixed by her toenails. There, inside the nails, in fractal complexity, were swirling galaxies, rotating solar systems, spinning planets, all expressions of life, all beings, all gods, all Brahmas, all Vishnus, all Shivas neatly contained within the smallest part of her! Swooning in ecstasy, the three gods, who were mere emanations of her will, hymned the Goddess for years and years on end.

In their adventure, the three greatest gods of India saw the absolute union of all things in the Goddess. They honored her as both eternal and non-eternal; She is both the deepest of all knowledge and the deepest of all illusion. If two things are actually one, were there ever two at all? If an actress plays Medea one night and Blanche DuBois the next, don't we recognize that the actress ultimately remains the same person? If the same divine force is both our knowledge and our ignorance, can we actually say that either exist? Brahma says to her, "If all those people laboring under the eightfold path of yoga, struggling always to achieve enlightenment, could just remember your name, they'd have the *moskha* they were striving for."

We categorize, we organize, we differentiate, because that's part of our nature – the nature given to us by the Goddess – but ultimately, we need to move beyond all of that and return to the one. Like Brahma, Vishnu and Shiva losing their manhood before the Goddess, we need to abandon our addiction to separatism in order to reach union with the Divine. We can't find the one while staring at two. There is no sacred. There is no profane. There is no good. There is no evil. There is no right. There is no wrong. There is no god. There is no devil.

Whenever I get into all of this during the course of a workshop or teacher training, someone inevitably – and rightly – raises the Hitler question.

"How can you say there's no evil? What about Hitler?" they ask. "We all know what he did was terrible."

People vigorously nod their heads and begin asking about other obvious atrocities we perpetrate upon each other – rape, child abuse, terrorism.

In answering the Hitler question, I often refer to a story that Elie Wiesel, Nobel Peace Prize-winning author and activist, used as the basis for his play *The Trial of God*. While a prisoner in Auschwitz, Wiesel witnessed a group of three learned rabbis put God on trial for his failure in protecting them from extermination. After many nights of hearing evidence, the men reached their verdict – Almighty God was guilty. Silence descended over this ersatz courtroom where the ashes of God's chosen people fell like snow on a winter landscape. Then, one of the rabbis looked heavenward and said, "It's time for evening prayers," and they began their nightly worship.

I always tell that story in response to these hard questions, not because I believe it will provide an answer, but because it leads us into a maze of inquiry about the nature of God. The politically correct answer in addressing any atrocious act against one person or many is to say, "This was just plain evil. God has nothing to do with it."

But I don't believe that. Hell, I don't believe in evil, either. The moments when I've been assaulted by cruelty, predation and intolerance both as a child and an adult haven't made me think there's a devil out there trying to get me. I've shaken my fist at the sky and cursed the gods, for sure, but I've come to think life is all some dark initiation into wisdom. If there is some underlying order to the cosmos – as there seems to be when we discover the Fibonacci sequence or the Theory of Relativity – then there is an underlying order even to chaos and destruction. Perhaps that order leads us into a greater understanding of what God is, beyond all images, personality, Thou Shalt Nots and mythical stories. Maybe that's where union really lies. Then again, maybe I'm going to a Calvinist hell when I die.

But I don't think so.

CHAPTER 3
THE DEVIL YOU KNOW

There will be times when we experience an essential union with all beings and God, but there will be many more times when we don't. Stuck in our habituation, we cling obsessively to what we know, despite the fact that what we know is destroying us. Take heart, though – eventually, our foolishness becomes our wake-up call. All the innocuous betrayals you perpetrate upon yourself every day are just *Maya* bringing you another step closer to enlightenment. In some of India's stories about the Goddess it's said that when fate turns against you, even a blade of grass becomes a thunderbolt. When we're completely mired in our delusions and idiocies, we don't even recognize those little moments that are actually harbingers of our downfall. We ignore a twinge of discomfort after a sticky conversation with a friend. We gloss over the bitchy comment our spouse made that hit uncomfortably close to something true. We refuse to listen to the quiet voice within that tells us not to do something we know is wrong. All these moments are the snowball that starts the avalanche.

The demons of India are famous for ignoring the voices that say, "Enough is enough." While here in the West, demons conjure up ghouls who torment poor sinners in a Dantean hell, that's not

really the case in India. The demons, the *asuras*, are the coun-
terpoint to the gods, the *devas*. They're a strong race of people
with an incredible capacity to achieve their desires. They'll work
and work and work to get what they want, and damn it, they're
going to have whatever they want because they deserve it. Being
demonic doesn't mean they're cast out from the spiritual realm.
In fact some of the greatest *tapasvas*, those who practice rigorous
austerities to gain a god's favor, are demons. However, once they
get God's attention, they usually ask for something that leads to
their downfall.

When a goddess says 'no,' she means it: Mahisasura was an immense,
powerful demon, half-human and half-buffalo, much like a cen-
taur. Born with an innate hatred of the gods, he performed an
epic *sadhana* to gain Brahma's favor. He chanted and chanted and
chanted for hundreds upon hundreds of years. He stopped eating altogether and just spent every moment focusing on the divine. The gods noticed his fervor and started to get nervous, so
they consulted with upper management, going to Brahma, and
asked him to visit the demon before the creature's accrued power
burned all of creation to cinders.

Brahma appeared before Mahisasura in a blaze of light, and
the demon, seeing the great one, prostrated himself on the earth.

"*Asura*, your practice is sublime. Tell me what I can give you in
return for your devotion."

"Great Creator, I want to be immortal."

"Ah, Mahisasura," sighed Brahma, "everything that is born
dies, even Vishnu, Shiva and myself. I do not have the power to
grant what you wish for. Ask me for something else."

The demon thought and then said, "Let only a woman be able
to kill me."

Surprised, Brahma said, "Done."

"All the worlds are now mine!" thought the demon, and rightly so. His prowess on the battlefield was as legendary as his *tapas*, so he knew that, for all intents and purposes, he had achieved immortality. No woman would dare challenge him to a fight, and now not even the mighty Vishnu could stand between him and world domination. Quickly, Mahisasura gathered an army of demons, all of whom bore no love for the treacherous gods, and with the great buffalo king at their head, they conquered all the worlds and routed the gods from heaven. Setting himself up on the throne of the king of the gods, Mahisasura ruled the entirety of creation. The fruit of every sacrifice went automatically to him, and he spent his days in sensual pleasures and the knowledge that his power was eternally secure.

The gods, after centuries of hiding in caves and remote valleys, had grown wan and despondent. Their heavenly kingdom and all of its delights were but a fading memory as they wandered through deserts, bathed themselves with frigid river water and ate tough roots dug up from an unyielding earth. Broken by their great ordeal, they went to Brahma for help.

"Great Creator," they said. "What can we do to win our kingdom back? How can we destroy Mahisasura?"

"Well, I gave him this boon that only a woman can kill him," Brahma said, and the gods swooned with grief. "Let's go to Shiva. He'll tell us what to do."

Traveling to Shiva's mountain abode, they found the ash-smeared ascetic in meditation and after gently awakening him, they laid their plight before him.

"That *is* tricky," grinned Shiva, then added, "We should see Vishnu. He always gets us out of these messes."

So, all the gods, including Brahma and Shiva, went to Vishnu's city, and again, they told their story.

"Hmmmmm," pondered the blue one. "There is nothing that Shiva or I can do," and after a long pause, he said, "Your only hope is Devi, the great Goddess. Worship her, and hopefully, she'll help us return creation to the ways of *dharma*."

All the gods, including the holy trinity of Brahma, Vishnu and Shiva, prayed to Devi, and after one thousand years of constant prayer, mantra and sacrifice, the beautiful one appeared before them. Her name was Durga, and she was so lovely and luminous that all of the gods fell on their faces before her, continuing to chant her mantras in ecstatic worship.

Finally, she raised her hand for them to stop and said in a voice as deep and seductive as the waves of the ocean, "Your devotion is exquisite. What can I do in return for such worship?"

"Devi," said Vishnu, with folded hands, "Mahisasura has taken over all the worlds, and creation has fallen into darkness. Holy men cannot do their sacrifices, the earth is withering and the cosmos is teetering on the brink of destruction. He has a boon that only a woman can kill him. Please save us."

With a glitter in her eye, Durga agreed and armed herself for battle. Each of the gods gave her their own weapons. On bended knee, Indra, the king of the gods, laid his mighty thunderbolt at her feet; Yama, lord of death, handed her his staff that could strike entire armies dead; the ocean god Varuna presented her with an unearthly lasso used to choke victims from afar; Shiva gladly offered her his flaming trident, and Vishnu, dazzled by her beauty, ceded to her the *sudarshana chakra*, a razor-sharp discus that none could stand against. Each of her eighteen arms held a god's weapon, and thus arrayed, she set out for battle.

Meanwhile, evil omens appeared around the palace of Mahisasura. Crows and vultures circled the battlements, stars fell screaming from the sky and an old gnarled hag wrapped in black rags was seen wandering the streets at midnight. One might think that any of these signs would raise some alarm in the demon king, but Mahisasura never even blinked. After all, nothing could destroy him, not even Vishnu!

Word came to him of a beautiful goddess, who had appeared on the earth riding on the back of a mighty lion, and instantly he was filled with a fiery lust to bed her. This was the kind of woman he'd been wanting as his queen – a resplendent Devi worthy of his greatness. He sent messengers with honeyed words to invite the woman to be his wife, but she rebuffed them, scoffed at his offer, mocked his looks and said, "Tell your master I've come for one reason and one reason only…"

The demon messengers leaned closer, as spellbound by her beauty and grace as their commander was.

"To kill him."

Quailing at having to deliver her words, the ambassadors crept back to Mahisasura and told him what she'd said. The mighty king of the *asuras* flew into a rage and commanded legion after legion to attack this lone woman. One by one, she razed them all in astounding displays of battle. Her mighty arms whirled at an uncanny speed, using the gods' weapons to extinguish thousands of demon warriors, and soon the battlefield was littered with corpses fed upon by crows, vultures and wild-eyed hyenas. At long last, Mahisasura himself came into battle, but when he saw her, love overtook him again and he tried, once more, to coax her into his bed.

"Oh, beautiful one," he said, sweetly, "you're not meant for all this death and battle. Why surround yourself with blood and filth when you should be doused in perfumes and wrapped in fine fabrics? Women are never truly happy without a husband, just as men are never truly happy without a wife. I offer you completion, fulfillment and love!" cried Mahisasura, becoming almost unhinged with his desire for her. "Come with me. Be my queen, and I'll be your slave. I'll do anything you ask – give up my fight with the *devas*, sit forever at your side, live anywhere, be anywhere. We'll be like Brahma with his Saraswati, Vishnu with his Lakshmi or Shiva with his Parvati. In fact, we'll be better than all of them, because I have vanquished every single one of them as you have vanquished me."

The Devi started to laugh, an intoxicating sound to Mahisasura, but her words cut him to the core. "I've killed countless demons before you and I'll kill countless others after you're dead. Your time has come. Leave this place and go to the underworld, or fight me and die."

Goaded by her arrogance and inflamed with passion, Mahisasura leapt into battle. The two fought a terrifying duel, hurling arrows and weapons that hadn't been seen in an age. Using his sorcery, Mahisasura changed forms – sometimes becoming a mighty lion, sometimes a raging buffalo – but all the while, the Goddess met him blow for blow, drinking wine and laughing while she relentlessly battled on. After nine days and nine nights, Durga grew so angry that she threw down all of the male gods' weapons, leapt onto Mahisasura's back and struck his head with her foot. He swooned from the blow, whereupon she picked up her sword and sliced off his head with the ease of a housewife cutting a carrot. While the gods rained flower petals down upon her, she carved off Mahisasura's horns and set them on her own head as a war trophy.*

It's never enough for the demons, and it's never enough for us. We want and we want and we want, and once we have, we want some more. It wasn't enough that Mahisasura actually saw God – he wanted to rule the world. Even that wasn't satisfying for him, because he knew what all of us know: nothing is eternal. Like everyone, he sought to put an infinite stamp on his reign, on his success, because none of us really wants to admit that all our hard work and good fortune will, one dark day, come completely unraveled and

---

* In the more popularly told versions of the fight, Mahisasura unseats the Goddess from her lion and begins kicking her, whereupon she severs his head with Vishnu's *sudarshana chakra*. The above telling, with Devi conquering the demon with her own innate power as opposed to the male gods' weapons, is told in rural communities.

leave us begging in the street. People play the stock market, riding high, putting their money into greater and greater opportunities, and then they're broke, living in a trailer park with no savings for the future. Someone is in a winning streak at their job, making sales, cutting deals, getting all the accolades until that new guy comes along and becomes the star of the show. You're a healthy person, at the gym, eating right, holding tight until you get a cancer diagnosis with a 50/50 chance of survival. The demon within wants to insure that our reign of pleasure and success never comes to an end, and we'll do whatever is necessary to make it happen. Work harder. Stay late at the job, the gym, school. Get another degree, another shot of botox, another hottie's phone number. Go the distance. That's what winners do. You work hard, you stay on top.

Until that blade of grass appears.

For Mahisasura, it was this magical woman, this one other thing he had to possess. There's nothing as alluring to our demonic selves as the unattainable. He sacrificed all his demon armies to get her, and when that didn't work, he lost himself to his own desire and pride. Never once did he look at what was happening around him, at all the blades of grass that were fast falling from the sky as thunderbolts, because he was so blinded by his own arrogance and stupidity. For us, the chase is what matters almost as much as the attainment of the goal, because that's when the blood gets pumping, that's when we fall into a whirling frenzy of dissatisfaction and fulfillment. One moment we think we have what we want – finally, at long last, *this* will make me happy– and the next we realize that there's something bigger and better out there, waiting for us to reach out and take it. It's a vicious cycle set in motion by no one else but us. The instant Mahisasura asks Brahma for the boon of being immortal to all but a woman, he's sealed his fate.

There are many Mahisasuras in the stories and in ourselves. The goddess Durga repeatedly appears to cleanse the world of some demon run amok, and the narrative is always the same: a demon wants to be immortal, Brahma says that's impossible, instead the demon asks to be killed only by a woman, he routs the gods, he takes over the worlds, the Devi appears at the gods' behest, the *asura* is dazzled by her beauty, she fights and destroys him. In some of the tales, the demon reaches *moksha* because he dies at her hands. The story repeats continuously because we continuously fall for the same tricks. We tell ourselves little and then grand lies to get us through the day or justify actions we know are dirty; those twisted moral acrobatics eventually rule us completely until Devi appears and ruins all our carefully, but incompletely, laid plans.

This is the other side of desire, the more classic side that teachers, gurus and priests warn against. Desire breeds dissatisfaction, arrogance and a skewed perspective that causes all the worlds within us to go awry. However, what we don't hear is that both the desires and the demons are leading us, inexorably, to God. Each demon who has conquered creation is undone by the Goddess' beauty. Each one wants to possess Her for himself, even though everyone around him warns him of the danger. He's still drawn to Her, because when it comes right down to it, the demons want to die. Death, in this sense, is a fulfillment, a cessation of all drives and endless wanting, and by consummating with Her (they think through lovemaking, but it's actually through sex's darker twin, death), they will come to the peace they've been searching for all along.

Whether a child fake tiptoes his way towards a forbidden cookie jar or a serial killer leaves an obvious trail for the authorities, the "bad" kid always wants to get caught. There's certainly a thrill in the chase and the daring of it all, but there's also a need to end the craziness going on inside. So many of us act out in a variety of ways to gain attention and censure for our behaviors. We, or the demonic parts of us, want to be destroyed.

Make no mistake about it: we're all harboring demons. Unfettered desire, a wish for domination (in the boardroom or the bedroom), an uncanny strength to achieve our goals no matter the cost, a palpable lust for fame – all these are symptoms of our demonic impulses, and in a culture that prizes an individual's manifest destiny above all else, these impulses have been given full rein. All our worlds – personal, interpersonal, economic, educational, political – have been hijacked by the demons. Greed is the order of the day, with cigar-smoking, corporate fat cats setting themselves up as the new emperors of the world. Politicians have lost all sense of true north on a wildly spinning moral compass, sacrificing lives for the sake of another term. The environment is burning at the hands of opportunistic financiers who act like idiot children playing with matches. Millions live on less than a dollar a day, while Westerners snap up cheap, plastic knickknacks at Wal-Mart with obscene glee, ignoring the children working long hours in substandard conditions in Asia to provide another Precious Moments figurine for an American's collection of crap. Rivers are poisoned to bring us more technology so we can ignore the state of the world around us, staring into a gadget making us dumber with each ping, clang and cricket chirp.

Some demon has certainly grabbed hold of us, and before it's all over, Big Mama is going to clean house. That's the way it has to happen. We are in a state of terrifying imbalance, and already the early stages of a cleanse are underway. It's a fact that the polar ice caps and glaciers are melting at unprecedented rates. It's a fact that the world is heating up and sea levels are rising. U.N. climate change reports have trumpeted the impending disaster with increasing panic, unveiling their findings that inevitable environmental catastrophe will lead to a worldwide human systems collapse. The gap between the classes is growing downright Dickensian and the discontent between them equally so. Yet, still, we are maniacally sawing away at our fiddles as Rome goes up in smoke. Even with thunderbolts dropping out of the heavens with alarming regularity, we carry on as if nothing is the matter, slaves to convenience and "progress," and if you think your membership in the yoga club absolves you from these sins, think again.

Vegetarianism for ecological reasons is a great choice (full disclosure: that's my reason for eating a vegetarian diet; that and my cowardice: if I can't slit the animal's throat myself, I have no business eating it), but what about all those great deals you find on clothes? Made in China, most likely by underage workers.

How wonderful that you're doing another juice cleanse! Did you walk by that homeless guy on the corner, ignoring his plea for money as you were sipping your eleven-dollar ginger-cucumber cocktail?

You're right – you *do* deserve a shopping spree at Lululemon because things at work have been really tough lately! Retail therapy and shopper-taining are your God-given American right! One wonders if those rooting through garbage dumps, fighting vermin off their food, feel the same elation when a new truck filled with fresher trash rolls up – what a great deal! Score!

Demons don't just appear in Disney villain costumes. It's not only our rage and cruelty that earn that monstrous moniker; our complicity is just as nasty a boogey-man. We all sacrifice ethical standing for convenience and consciously turn a blind eye to the suffering of the world around us just to "get it done." That "it" can be a work project, a personal goal or an item to buy. We do this with our yoga, as well. As an industry, we in the yoga world spend *millions* on supplies (and, really, what more do you need besides your body and the earth itself to practice on?), redundant teacher trainings and yoga conferences. We practice in gingham-accented pants that cost over $100, taking breaks from a pose to sip reverse-osmosis water we bought at a chichi market and then pull on our Uggs (made from sheep tormented in unbelievable cruelty) before rushing back to the office, texting away on the most recent iWhatever.

The stories of India say that when the gods decide to break someone, first they take away their intelligence, their ability to discriminate between what's true and what's not. When we lose that capacity, we fall prey to the demons inside us. We're so wrapped up in ignorance that we can't even recognize our hypocrisies and psychological double-speak, and that's where the real danger lies. It's not that all this yogic practice allows us to wipe out the race of demons. They'll always be there; there will always be parts of us that we label as unsavory. What yoga does is grant us the gift of sight. Now we can *see* the big, scaly, horned beastie skulking around the edges of the room, and once we see him, his sneak attack is far less of an ambush.

Demons only take over when the gods swell with pride, so they teach the lords of light some well-deserved humility. Sometimes we get lucky. Sometimes other gods do the work of the demons, alerting us to our arrogance before an all-out war between the forces of light and darkness, forever at odds within us.

From the mouths of babes: Indra is the king of the *devas*. There's a certain level of god that Indra rules – the deities of wind, ocean, fire, death and other natural forces – and he's a powerful king, somewhat similar to the Greek pantheon's Zeus (however, Brahma, Vishnu, Shiva and, of course, Devi outrank him). Indra once killed a particularly nasty demon, and he was feeling very proud of himself, indeed. In celebration of his efforts, he decided to build a spectacular palace, so he asked Viswakarman, the architect of the gods, to craft something really unique for him. Viswakarman outdid himself and began building an astonishing creation, but as with all building projects, the buyer had his own ideas. Indra was constantly nagging Viswakarman about a new fountain he wanted, a bigger dining hall, a grander throne room with greater statues.

Almost driven mad by the changing demands, Viswakarman went to Vishnu for help.

"Great Lord, Indra is out of control," sighed an exhausted Viswakarman. "This palace he wants is too much. Can you please do something to quell his demands?"

The blue god smiled languidly at the memory of something Viswakarman couldn't possibly have known and assured the builder he'd take care of it. The next day at the construction site, Indra was poring over new plans he'd drawn up in the night when suddenly a small, vibrantly blue boy arrived. He was rapturously beautiful, and Indra stared at him as the child looked around at the progress, nodding his head here and there or clapping his hands delightedly, almost as if he'd seen it all before.

The boy walked right up to Indra, who still was gazing fondly at his blue skin, and said, "This is, indeed, better than all the other palaces built by all the other Indras before you."

The king of the gods snapped out of his reverie. "What did you say?"

Smiling bewitchingly, the child responded, "Your palace. I think it truly is better than all the other palaces built by all the other Indras before you."

"What other Indras?" the slayer of demons and wielder of thunderbolts stammered.

"Oh, you don't know about them? Let me explain," and the child sat disarmingly on the floor, inviting Indra to do the same. "Brahma, the creator, sits atop a lotus flower that grows from the navel of Lord Vishnu. Brahma opens his eyes and a world is created with its own set of gods, its own demons and its own Indra, who kills a particularly nasty monster and then sets about building a mighty palace in celebration. Brahma closes his eyes and that world is destroyed and with it, its own set of gods, its own demons, its own Indra and the palace he built as a trophy." Indra had gone very pale, yet the child, seemingly oblivious to the king's discomfort, pressed on. "On and on this goes. Brahma opens his eyes, another world, another Indra. He closes his eyes, they're all destroyed. Eventually, after innumerable worlds come and go, even Brahma himself dies and the lotus stalk shrivels, too. Time passes in ages uncountable, and then, another lotus grows from the navel of Vishnu, another Brahma finds himself sitting atop it and he begins opening and closing his eyes."

Just at this point, when Indra thought he'd heard more than enough, a large troop of ants came marching into his newly risen palace. They were a seemingly infinite number and arranged neatly, like soldiers marching into battle. The blue boy smirked – some would say impishly – gestured toward the ants and said, "Former Indras all."

We think we're so special, and we're often told as much, if not from childhood then by a culture obsessed with the cult of celebrity and being noticed. (Facebook! Instagram! Twitter! Look at me! I'm fascinating!) Everyone is trying to make a mark and be validated for their looks, their opinions, even what they had for lunch. We want to believe we're unique, that we're not only the best Indra, but that there were no other Indras before us, and once we fall into this trap, the demons start their *tapas*, diligently working towards unlimited power and domination. The gods have grown haughty, and this is their downfall.

Our mistake isn't in aligning ourselves with "godly" ways. Our mistake is believing those ways are better than everyone else's. The *devas* cheat, lie, sleep around and murder just like the demons do, so much so that, at times, it's hard to tell who's good and who's bad. Certain demons are more holy than the gods, and certain gods are crueler than the demons. Sometimes the demons win the day, sometimes the gods, and so it goes with us. Inside all of us are an entire set of gods and demons fighting for dominance over the worlds that are our body, our mind, our heart and our soul, and as long as we continue to venerate one and denigrate the other, we will be forever caught in the crossfire.

Sri Ramakrishna, a great Indian saint and mystic of the 1800s, was believed to be an avatar of God, and he was a devotee of the goddess Kali. While teaching, he spontaneously composed poetry dedicated to Her, sang sacred songs to the goddess and fell into such deep trances that his devotees had to carry him from one location to the other. He often horrified his disciples when he leapt out of carriages to prostrate himself fully before toothless prostitutes in the streets. He saw no difference between them and Kali. He had moved beyond the parsing of people into "good" and "bad," god and demon, and discovered the true transcendent, yet pervasive, unity that runs through all of life.

He said, "I prayed to the Divine Mother only for love. I offered flowers at Her Lotus Feet and said with folded hands: 'O Mother, here is Thy ignorance and here is Thy knowledge; take them both and give me only pure love for Thee. Here is Thy holiness and here is Thy unholiness; take them both and give me only pure love for Thee. Here is Thy virtue and here is Thy sin; here is Thy good and here is Thy evil; take them all and give me only pure love for Thee. Here is Thy *dharma* and here is Thy *adharma*; take them both and give me only pure love for Thee.'

"*Dharma* means good actions, like giving in charity. If you accept *dharma*, righteousness, you have to accept *adharma*, unrighteousness, too. If you accept virtue, you have to accept sin. If you accept knowledge, you have to accept ignorance. If you accept holiness you have to accept unholiness. It is like a man's being aware of light, in which case he is aware of darkness, too. If a man is aware of one, he is aware of many, too. If he is aware of good, he is aware of evil, too.

"Blessed is the man who retains his love for the Lotus Feet of God even though he eats pork."

If we are to believe that God is all things, no exceptions, then we can no longer say "God is good." We can truly only come up with "God Is." Good, bad, indifferent, it's all part of the divine impulse radiating throughout this creation. Yes, God is found in a blossoming garden, the birth of a child and falling in love, but God is also found in tsunamis, starvation, madness and grief.

If we cling to the notion that God is good, we're immediately thrown into turmoil when life turns out to be shitty and a benevolent God is allegedly at the helm. When a woman is raped, what cruel idiot would dare say to her, "Well, God is good, and as all things come from God, this, too, was good"? When a child is murdered, how can we even think that this is "good"? When war ravages a people, we don't have the right to quip piously about God's ultimate kindness. The words die in our throats, because it doesn't gel with our experience. If we try to maintain the notion of God's "goodness" in the face of devastation, we've just given birth to an army of demons, who cry out, quite rightly, "Bullshit!" Duality is fostered within us and the call to war is sounded. As long as the *devas* keep ignoring what the *asuras* are saying, we'll always be trapped in the kind of duality Ramakrishna was talking about. Just as surely as the gods, our demons are driving us towards our ultimate awakening.

Under the sea: There was a time when the gods themselves were losing their immortality, not a good situation given the propensity of the demons to declare war on the *devas*. The anxious heavenly host asked Vishnu what to do, and languidly, he replied, "Go and churn the ocean of milk. The *amrita*, the nectar of immortality, lies beneath its waves, and it will restore your immortal luster. Use Mount Mandara as the churning stick and ask Vasuki, king of the divine serpents, to be the rope wound round the mountain for the churning. You'll also have to ask for the demons' help in the matter. Only they are strong enough to haul the other end of Vasuki."

The gods began to protest, but Vishnu held up one of his hands. "Indra, go to them. Feign friendship. Promise them some of the *amrita* in reward for their efforts, and above all, be humble! I'll make sure they don't get any of the sacred nectar. Go."

Indra did, indeed, visit the demons to tell them about the joint venture, and he was nothing but sweet and obsequious before his age-old adversaries. At the promise of *amrita*, the demons readily agreed to help their enemies with the churning of the ocean, and soon, the *devas* and *asuras* hefted Mount Mandara above their heads and dropped it in the center of the milky sea. Both races went to Vasuki, king of the ancient wise serpents, and after promising him a share of the *amrita*, they convinced him to be used as a hauling rope for the churning. They wound Vasuki around the mountain, but just as the *devas* began to take up their positions at Vasuki's head, the demons set up a ruckus.

"What is this? We deserve the honor of pulling him by the head. Let the proud *devas* take the tail. They came to us, after all!"

Indra's temper began to flare, but Vishnu shot him a look, reminding him to be humble and the king of the gods led his people to Vasuki's tail. Each team picked up their end of the mighty serpent, and they started pulling back and forth. The mountain began spinning, and the ocean of milk soon grew frothy. Nothing more happened for some time, and both *deva* and *asura* began to tire. They called out to Vishnu for help, and seeing that the mountain needed steadying, the blue one transformed a part of himself into a large turtle that wedged itself under the twisting peak. The gods and demons renewed their pulling, which was all the more powerful now that the Vishnu turtle was steadying Mandara's base, and each time the mountain whirled on its back, the turtle giggled with ticklish delight.

Again, the ocean frothed, and again, the gods and demons began to flag. Vishnu, because he was God and not relegated to one form, stood above Mandara and held its peak down with the palm of his hand to steady it even more. The teams started pulling harder and faster now, and the ocean's waves grew wilder with each rush of the mountain. Noticing that the *devas* just weren't as strong as the demons, Vishnu adopted a third form and joined the gods' efforts at the serpent's tail.

By this time, poor Vasuki was so dizzy that he felt ill and with Vishnu's mighty strength added to the pulling, the great serpent king started vomiting fiery poison right into the faces of the demons who'd been so adamant about grabbing the serpent's head. Vishnu grinned and kept hauling, but the smile died on his lips as he saw various creatures of the deep come swimming frantically to the top of the ocean as if they were fleeing a great danger. In fact, they were and in a flash Vishnu dropped Vasuki's tail, and cried, "Quick! Fly to Lord Shiva! He's the only one who can save us now! The *halahala* is rising from the depths of the ocean, and if left unchecked it will destroy all of creation!"

The *devas* were horrified at the mere mention of the *halahala*, the most dreadful poison in all the universe, and they were equally frightened by Vishnu's awful anxiety. Led by the blue god, the *devas* fled to Mount Kailash, the abode of Shiva, who, as usual, was meditating calmly when the frantic gods arrived. He slowly opened his eyes and said, "You seem to be in a terrible fright. Even you, Vishnu. Tell me what brings you to the mountain."

"Great One," said Vishnu, breathlessly, "the *halahala* has risen from the ocean of milk. You are the only one who can save the world from this danger."

Shiva's love Parvati stood at his side, and he could tell without looking at her that she was not pleased by the idea, yet Shiva never could resist those in need, so he agreed to help them. Quick as thought, he stood in the frothy white ocean and quaffed the poison, and although he did rescue creation from annihilation, the *halahala* was so potent that it burned Shiva's throat blue, earning him the nickname *nilakantha*, the blue-throated one.

Saved from destruction, the gods and demons resumed their work, and soon enough, untold wonders emerged from the ocean. Both the great *Kamadhenu*, the beautiful divine cow who grants all wishes, and the *Kalpavriksha*, a radiant wish-fulfilling tree, rose from its waves. Other precious objects and beings came from the depths, and finally, Dhanvantari, the physician of the gods, arrived holding the pot of sacred *amrita*. The gods and demons fell back in wonder at the sight, but even the famous *amrita* was nothing compared to what came next.

The resplendent goddess of abundance and beauty, Lakshmi, floated to the white surface of the ocean of milk. She was completely naked and seated in a radiant lotus flower. God and demon alike were awestruck by her beauty, some even had tears in their eyes at the sheer indescribable loveliness of her. It seemed that the world had never known anything beautiful before she came into being, and indeed, it had not. The unparalleled goddess stood up from her floral throne, and her body was a dream of sweetness and seduction. Milk ran over her naked curves like fresh rain cascading down the sides of a mountain, and her eyes swept the motley assembly of exhausted *devas* and *asuras* until her gaze alighted on Vishnu. Passionate fires of love kindled in her eyes, and Vishnu was almost beside himself with longing for his *shakti*, the consort that he knew was his other half as soon as she crested the waves. She walked over to him, her hips swaying and her eyes full, and she laid a garland of blooming flowers around his neck, claiming the blue preserver of the cosmos as her very own.

After Vishnu wrapped Lakshmi in his arms and a contented smile spread across his handsome face, the *devas* and *asuras* snapped back to attention and the matter at hand: the *amrita*! They both began arguing over who was to have it first and a battle threatened to break out, a battle with unknown consequences as both peoples were formidable warriors. Suddenly and very unexpectedly, a gorgeous woman appeared in their midst. She was a dark blue color, her hair was luxurious and her body something out of legend. Both the gods and the demons stopped their squabbling and stared at this raven-haired beauty who moved so seductively, her every gesture an invitation to ravish her! She glanced at the demons and raised an eyebrow – after all, the *asuras'* endless stamina on the battlefield translated equally to the bedroom – and she looked at the *devas* and gave a curious wink, like a schoolboy playing a prank. Not exactly sure what was happening, Indra gestured to his men to fall back from the enchantress whose name was Mohini.

She picked up the pot of *amrita* and sidled over to the demons. In a breathy voice and with a conspiratorial look, she said "Let me serve the *devas* first and get them out of the way. Then you can have the rest of the *amrita* and," she dropped her voice to a whisper, "perhaps the rest of me." The demons fell over themselves agreeing with her, and off she flitted to the gods, doling out *amrita* to each one of them.

There was one demon, however, who wasn't buying it. He sensed a trick in the offing and being a master of sorcery, he disguised himself as a god and joined the *devas'* line. Mohini poured a draught for the Sun and then gave a cup to the disguised demon, Rahu, who stood innocently between the Sun and the Moon. The two luminaries alerted Mohini to the deception, and quick as a flash she revealed herself to be who she really was: Vishnu! With his whirling *sudarshana chakra*, he hewed off the demon's head before the *amrita* made it down his throat, and Rahu's head flew into the cosmos, forever immortal, where it periodically devours the Sun and Moon in punishment for their betrayal.

Vishnu instantly resumed his form as Mohini, and giggling naughtily, finished serving the *devas* until there was nothing left of the *amrita*. As Mohini turned back towards the *asuras*, Vishnu revealed himself, and the demons roared in rage at the *devas'* treachery. They picked up their weapons and rushed the gods, determined to make an end of the deceivers, but with the *amrita* coursing through their veins, the *devas* quickly beat the demons back, slaying entire legions of them. The surviving stragglers fled to the netherworlds to nurse their wounds, recover their losses and bitterly plan their next assault.

This story is much more than a "primitive" explanation of where eclipses come from. The pact between the *devas* and the *asuras*, the churning, the revelation from the depths of the ocean are all happening within us, all the more so if we're conscious of it. At any given time, we are pulled back and forth by our "good" and "bad" impulses. We want to go out to the party/we told our parents we'd go to dinner with them tonight. We should save our bonus for home repairs/we want to blow it all on a weekend in New York. The plain Jane or Bob has their shit together and is a really nice match for us/the hot Scott or Nina is kind of a mess but way more fun in the sack. Torn apart by endless motivations to do the right or wrong thing (read: what we're told is right vs. what feels right), our inner sea is churned.

Over years, this frothing seems to leave us only with a messy ocean, unless we become conscious of the process. Through yoga or therapy or meditation, we look at what's going on inside of us and choose to be more aware of the back-and-forth. We steady the mountain of our effort, which only allows us to work harder, with more opportunities for churning coming left and right. The back-and-forth of life's big choices is accented by our new ability to see the little conundrums as practice runs for the larger dramas. How we treat our pets, our responsibilities at our job, even cleaning our home triggers a tug-of-war about what we want versus what we should want. Now, the seas get rough with all the extra attention, and we start blaming all those bad tendencies, all those demons within us, for our problems. Belching poisonous fire at them we project all of our bad choices onto some terrible, innate proclivities within us – lust, anger, resentment, pride, whatever your bugaboos are.

Soon after, with all this interior work, our darkest materials reveal themselves. Meditation and yoga surely lead to some sense of wholeness, but that's only after the *halahala* of your own twisted nightmares and traumas comes boiling to the surface. We finally see that we haven't been betrayed by others or by the "demons" – we've actually betrayed ourselves. That string of relationships gone wrong? You knew what the problems were from the get-go, but you chose not to see them. The years of torment you experienced as an adult at the hands of your family? You let it happen because you kept quiet about it. The dream deferred because you didn't have the money, or the time, or the support? You were just too scared to go for it; the risk to your portfolio was too great. Yoga brings us to this – it brings us face-to-face with the betrayals we've perpetrated upon ourselves but blamed on others. It releases the poisons we've held back for years, deep within our consciousness, and those recognitions will utterly destroy all sense of who we are.

Perhaps, in all of the fear and devastation at revealing the *halahala* of our psyche, we come to a point where we can handle it. We actually swallow the poison, we assimilate it back into ourselves, change our lives and behavior, recognizing that this isn't anyone's problem but our own. We also know that like a homeopathic medicine, the deadly poison of our ignorance actually contains our healing. That doesn't mean that wrangling the toxic past doesn't take its toll. We all get burned by that, but the burn, the blue scar, is a potent reminder of our present courage and our former weakness.

Finally, after all of that work comes the miracle. Boons and gifts rise from within, and the precious nectar of immortality, which has been waiting there all along as a curative for the madness that ails us, is ours. Beyond even that comes ultimate beauty, abundance and bliss. The *Devi*, the Goddess, emerges from our psyche, and what we've been searching for all our lives, a sense of completion, is in our grip; for beyond all notions of immortality, we want to be whole. We crave the knowledge that there's no more searching to be done, that we've arrived. The torment of ceaseless wanting can finally be put to rest, because the fulfillment of all desire has just been born from within us. We wed those two parts of ourselves together, Vishnu and Lakshmi, and finally, we're free. We are content in and with ourselves.

This can only come about, though, *because* of the friction between the *devas* and the *asuras* who lurk inside, and this is the real meaning of *tapas*. In yoga, *tapas* is the friction caused by heat, a kind of heat that purifies, and while doing certain *asanas* can generate a literal heat, it's the *tapas* we do in our daily lives which churns our consciousness. Every time you want one thing but get another, that's *tapas*. When you lose an argument, *tapas*. When you have to subvert your will for someone else's, definitely *tapas*. Driving? *Tapas*. Work? *Tapas*. Relationships? The best *tapas* there is. If we're just bandied about by the opposing forces within us, then we're more poor, old Vasuki than Vishnu and Lakshmi. If we can actually see what's going on, if, during an argument with a spouse, we are aware of the tug-of-war inside of us and we speak from that recognition, then the gods and the demons are working together to create something new.

And what of Mohini? Who are the real villains in this story? The gods were bent on trickery from the get-go, with Indra blithely lying through his teeth to use up the demons' strength in the churning. All the *devas* played along when Vishnu did his Mohini drag show, drinking up the *amrita*, despite their promises to share. Isn't honesty a quality we associate with the godly, with the beings made of light? Why is it that when dealing with demons, the very first race created by Brahma, we criticize their every misstep, but we turn a blind eye to the gods' deceit?

Luckily, there's always one demon inside of us who sees through our own bullshit. He knows better than to trust those lying goody-goodies, nor is he interested in the usual seductions of wine, women and song. There's something greater at stake here, and he's going to go for the brass ring. We all have a Rahu within us. He's the doubter, the one who's never, ever satisfied, who urges us to go higher and farther than seems possible, to reach past the station put upon us by the ones in control, whether they are our own repressive thoughts or a cultural code of ethics constructed to serve Puritanical nonsense to a dim-witted public. The Rahu impulse within us is immortal, having tasted the *amrita*, so that voice will always exist, forever challenging our *devic* impulses.

For the time being, though, the demons are beaten back, and the gods are sitting pretty in their palace. We feel vindicated, we feel as if we've really got it now – until we go too far and the next demon comes along to send us all to hell. On and on it goes, this battle, this churning, this search for immortality. *That* will never, ever cease, and perhaps it's not intended to. Notice that Vishnu doesn't kill all of the demons, as he certainly could, but instead lets them go, setting in motion a future vendetta with the gods, another opportunity to break ourselves asunder and plunge ever deeper into the ocean of who we are.

CHAPTER 4

CURTAIN UP!

B oth the gods and the demons have their own precious domains –
the *devas* live in heaven and the *asuras* in the underworld – and as
all these worlds exist inside of us, in the course of a lifetime we spend
stints in both. Despite all appearances to the contrary, yoga doesn't
help us secure a place in the garden of paradise, but actually sends us
kicking and screaming into the dark caverns of our own hell. These
days, yoga has joined the proselytizing ranks of all the other American
get-well-quick schemes with studios across the country capitalizing on
the great hope that is the yogic path. Yoga will cure your arthritis/
depression/diabetes/high blood pressure/meth addiction/goiters! All
you have to do is start practicing, stay committed and your troubles will
vanish like the mist at dawn.

Yet no one tells you that some days, yoga sucks. It's an ordeal
just to get on the mat. We'd rather be watching TV, reading, eating, anything else but carving out time to focus on the craziness
that's going on inside our own heads, and if you're still one of those
people caught up in the "yoga will always make you feel better"
propaganda, then you're not being honest with yourself. Plenty of
instructors make it their goal to get people feeling good, shovel-
ing happy horseshit down everyone's throats – all students should

leave the room with a smile! – but the truth is that's not where yoga is taking us. Yoga might eventually lead us to heaven, but it's only after traveling the rocky road through hell. The sooner we all take out the ear buds piping us full of new age platitudes and look at the lake of fire blazing outside the bus window, the better off we'll be. If we don't, if we spend all of our time avoiding the dark nastiness we carry, then we're fad-following fools. That's okay, though, because the bus goes to hell whether we're singing nursery rhymes along the way or screaming in terror, but to learn the lessons from the underworld that we need, it's far more productive to embrace our destination.

Bhaktas gone bad: Vishnu has two gatekeepers, Jaya and Vijaya, who stand guard outside his glorious abode, and they are deeply devoted to their lord. They love him endlessly and being in his presence is all they desire. One day, four sages come to visit Vishnu, and as they approach Vishnu's home, the gatekeepers stop the four wanderers.

"Vishnu cannot be seen now," says Jaya, holding up a hand.

"The Lord is resting," adds Vijaya, also blocking the sages' way.

The visitors are so angry at being rejected that they curse Jaya and Vijaya to be born as mortals on earth and go through the cycles of life and death. The gatekeepers are absolutely despondent, and when Vishnu awakens, they mournfully tell him everything.

"I cannot lift their curse entirely," he says, "but I can make it easier. You have a choice. Either you can each live seven lives on earth as my devotees, or you can each live three as my bitterest enemies. At the end of your prescribed incarnations, you'll return to me forever."

Jaya and Vijaya didn't need to think long at all. They'd rather be Vishnu's dire enemies and get this all over with quickly, instead of singing his praises and spending a longer time away from the great one. The pair goes on to incarnate as some of the worst fiends in Hindu myth, and each time they do, Vishnu appears as an avatar to slay them.

First comes the demon Hiranyaksha, who plunges the earth into the depths of a mighty ocean, and Vishnu incarnates as a monstrous boar, carrying the earth to the surface before goring the demon to death. Next is the *asura* Hiranyakashipu. He absolutely loathes Vishnu and performs an unparalleled *tapas* to gain the boon of immortality. Of course, that's impossible, but he is granted that no man or beast can kill him day or night, inside or outside, on the earth or in the sky. In order to dodge the boon and slay the demon, Vishnu incarnates as the terrifying Narasimha, part man and part lion. The great god kills the demon on the threshold of a doorway at twilight while balancing him on his thighs and tearing him apart with his claws. The famous Ravanna of the Ramayana epic and his brother Kumbhakarna are both killed by Vishnu's form of Rama, and finally Krishna slays two kings, Dantavakra and Sishupal, during his legendary incarnation. After these final villains are killed, Jaya and Vijaya return to Vishnu's side, never to leave it again.

Two divine beings willingly become absolute devils, because they're desperate to return to God's side. As these inimical incarnations, they do terrible things – destroy the planet, torture the innocent, rape women, murder babies – yet Jaya and Vijaya happily pay that price in order to get back to Vishnu. The pair races into the depths of hell to win God's eternal favor.

We're told in our likely Judeo-Christian home traditions and in the new wisdom we're discovering in yoga to sublimate, sidestep and override any "negative" tendencies we carry within ourselves. We're encouraged to be the good kids, because that sounds a lot nicer than being the schoolyard bully or part of the gang that smokes under the bleachers. Those types are losers, they always get in trouble and they'll never get anywhere in life – at least that's the narrative our society has about the rejects - so, instead we play by the rules handed down to us. We study, get good grades, date the right person, go to the best school, get a good job, work our way up. We marry the person everybody says is perfect for us, and we have children. We go to church or synagogue or yoga class and follow their rules, too, because all of this teaches us how to be good people, and good people always win the game, right?

Not really.

Life is not a vending machine where we put in our money, press B2 and get a Snickers bar. Usually, the candy gets stuck in the capricious wire claw of fate, and while the good kids go to the hall monitor and then the janitor and then the facilities manager for help, the bad kids have already broken the glass and grabbed Snickers, Reese's Pieces and a few Hostess cupcakes for good measure.

Funny thing about the rejects: they're always thinking about the very thing that's rejecting them. The straitlaced crowd rests on the laurels of their achievements, but the punks are figuring out ways to subvert the system, screw the authorities and get away with their schemes. This takes a lot of focus on "the man"; they're completely obsessed with the people who have done them wrong, and so it was with Jaya and Vijaya in their demonic incarnations. They harbored a burning hatred for Vishnu, and this passion consumed their every moment. They railed against him publicly or nursed secret anxieties in the night, doing everything in their power to overcome the Blue One. The demons literally go to their deaths thinking of God – whether he appears as Narasimha, Rama or Krishna – and therefore achieve *moksha*.

In some ways, the actions we take in this life don't matter. *Karma* is an electric fence used to keep the cows in place. We carefully avoid anything that smacks of "bad" behavior, because we know – or rather, we've been told – that what goes around comes around. You do good things now, you get good things later (a terribly selfish motivation for doing good works). You do bad things now, you inevitably get punished later. Is that true, though? Remember Jaya and Vijaya. Remember the five Pandava brothers and the battlefield where millions are slain in terrible violence. It's Vishnu himself, speaking as Krishna, who says in the *Bhagavad Gita* that once a person reaches enlightenment, *karma* has no hold on them. It falls away from us completely, and there will be no more cosmic accounting for our good or bad deeds.

Perhaps *karma* only works because of our ignorance. Without understanding that we *are* God and God *is* us, we bind ourselves to a tit-for-tat polarity. We're tricked into thinking (by no one but ourselves) that we do something to someone else, instead of knowing that there is no one but God. There is no slayer or slain, as Krishna says in the *Gita*. If we believe in duality, in complete separateness between ourselves and others, then the law of *karma* takes hold in our psyche and we're caught. "She did this to me! What a bitch! I'll never forgive her!" "Oh, I can't believe I did that to them. I'm such a shit. I'll never forgive myself." Instead of *karma* being some invisible web in which we're hopelessly tangled, *karma* is a product of our own mind. Liberate yourself from the mind, and *karma* is revealed as the cheap theatrics of ignorance.

Our entire existence is theater put on by God who is scriptwriter, director, set maker and actor. So often, we think the Divine is just the puppeteer, making us dance to an off-key calliope and then sitting by uselessly when the comedy turns to tragedy. But possibly, God is all of it, directing Itself in the starring role – the protagonist being each one of us – because it's fun. God gets to feel, to love, be loved, go mad with rage, cower in terror, experience the ecstasies of overwhelming joy and shattering sorrow. God is everything, so God is the drama and every component of it, as well.

Any actor will tell you about the sweet intoxication of going to the limits of a human life, of feeling the tragedy of Hamlet and the comedy of Bottom as if they're his very own. That's why actors return again and again to the stage, even with all the difficulty it creates in the "real world" of money, relationships and stability. They want to live the infinite varieties of human experience from Shakespeare to Beckett.

The problem is not with the theater itself but when we believe we are that character. If an actor didn't stop playing the melancholy Dane after the final act of *Hamlet*, we'd say he has a problem and suggest therapy, but this is the very madness we're all actually living. Every day we get wrapped up in the drama without keeping a piece of ourselves steady in the notion that there's a stage door just beyond the wings. There's a peaceful world out there where no characters will punish us for our transgressions or reward us for our victories, where no future plans are laid, where there are no effects because there are no causes. Once we recognize that we're just in a play, ultimately unaffected by twists of plot and character, the game changes entirely. Now, we chew the scenery because it's fantastic theater; as the ancient Greeks knew, drama actually keeps us sane and holds the very stars in their place.

⇌⇌

Something in the water: The sage Narada is one of the great mystic figures of Hindu myth. A legendary *rishi* and Vishnu *bhakta*, he was once cursed to forever wander the cosmos, never resting for too long in any one place. One day he was walking with Vishnu, and the pair was talking about the nature of existence.

"Does *Maya* really hold sway over the cosmos?" asked Narada.

In response, Vishnu taught the sage about the nature of life and had a good laugh at the same time. They walked to the edge of a lake, and the god casually suggested the *rishi* take a dip, which he gladly did on that warm day, stripping off all his clothes and diving into the crystalline waters. When he emerged moments later, Vishnu was gone, and Narada was actually no longer Narada but a beautiful naked woman! The sage had no memory of being a great *rishi*, traveler of the highest realms of heaven and devoted to the beautiful blue preserver of creation; this woman only knew that she remembered nothing before emerging from the lake. Dazed, she sat on its banks and wondered what was to become of her.

The pounding of horse hooves reached her ear, and in a moment, a handsome, powerfully built warrior emerged from the jungle. He saw her naked, buxom body glistening with lake water in the sun, and he swung down off his horse and nearly babbled before her.

"Beautiful woman, or are you even human? You must be some divine being, a heavenly dancer or courtesan dropped down from the realm of the gods. Tell me, who is your family? Where are you from?"

"Sir," she said, trying to hide her blush, for she was overwhelmed with desire for the stranger, "I know it sounds impossible, but I don't know how I got here. I don't know my name, my people or my birthplace. I only remember coming out of the water, and I've been sitting here for hours trying to figure out what to do."

Without hesitation, the warrior said, "Be mine! My blood is on fire for you, and I promise to treat you as the goddess you are. I am a king, and I will take you back to my palace and make you my queen."

Stunned by her good fortune and desirous to be in this king's strong arms, she agreed; he covered her with some of his own garments before lifting her onto his horse and galloping back to the royal city. Quickly, they married, and as soon as the ceremony was finished, they retired to the royal apartments for days of lovemaking. Although she didn't remember anything of her life before, the king's new wife certainly knew the arts of love, coaxing him deeper into her until they both shuddered with pleasure. Eventually, the king tore himself away from his queen and returned to ruling the kingdom, but the royal pair's nights were lit by the fires of passion.

In time, she became pregnant and bore him a son and then more sons after the heir. Their children grew, the kingdom was awash in peace, and the couple's love only deepened. When the boys were full-grown, their mother helped them find wives of their own, and soon, there were grandchildren running about the palace, reminding the queen of the sweet days when her own children laughed without worry and cried over trifles.

One day a rival king sent an emissary to the court and declared war. The queen's husband and sons gathered a royal army, riding out to meet the villain's challenge. Days of battle ensued, and during the war, the rival king killed all of the queen's children and eventually routed the king himself in battle. When he returned in despair to the city, telling her what had happened, she became unhinged – screaming, sobbing, shaking her fists at the gods and clawing the ground in agony. She'd lost everything, all of her precious babies. Soon the barbarians would breach the gates to slay the grandchildren and rape the city's women.

In the midst of her grief, a wandering, decrepit holy man came to the royal chambers and said to her, "During such devastation, only a pilgrimage to sacred waters will soothe you, your highness. There is one close to the city. Shall I take you there?"

For the first time in days, she was calmed. She instantly trusted this stranger, although she couldn't say why.

"Lead the way," she said.

She followed the old man out of the royal apartments, past the city gates and into the forest. Sheltered by the boughs of trees, the old one told her about the nature of existence and how all things are born to die.

"Sorrow inevitably follows joy," he said wistfully, "and nothing ever belongs to us permanently. Only *Brahman*, the Eternal One, has any stability. Seek That and know peace."

They reached the waters of the holy lake, and she stripped off her queenly garments. Her clothes pooled at her feet as she stepped into the cool waters. She looked back once at the holy man who had an odd lopsided grin on his face, but thinking nothing more of it, she walked into the water's depths.

As the cooling waves lapped at her aging body, her husband arrived, having heard from an old townswoman where the queen had gone and with whom. He stood silently while the queen submerged herself entirely, but gasped aloud when a glowing rishi emerged from beneath the surface where once his queen had been. Narada had returned! The sage stared disbelievingly around him, blinking the water from his eyes, and quickly glanced down at his body to see the familiar man's form. He looked up at the shore and saw the shocked king and a laughing Vishnu in place of the holy man.

When Narada walked out of the water, still in absolute wonder at what had transpired, the king began running up and down the edge of the lake, almost hysterical.

"Where is my queen, my love?" he cried. "I've lost everything, my kingdom, my children, I cannot lose her. I'll take my own life!"

Assuming the guise of the holy man again, Vishnu told him the same things he'd told Narada/the queen about the way of existence, and he urged him to go seek peace at one of the many ashrams in the jungle. As the king stumbled deep into the forest to find a save haven for his storm-wrecked soul, Vishnu again started to laugh.

"I didn't remember who I was," Narada said, and then added, somewhat ashamed, "I didn't even remember you."

"This is the nature of life," Vishnu chuckled, "This is *Maya*."

It's all a show. It's all a story. We come here with certain parts to play, scripts in hand, and almost without being able to help it, we step onto the stage and tell the tale. Just as an actor isn't really

King Lear, so Narada wasn't really the queen to a mighty king, yet, while on stage, he committed fully to each moment, each turn of fate. The sage had hot sex, reared children, sobbed hysterically at their loss – he did everything to the highest heights and the lowest lows.

This is what life asks of us, and if we don't engage it, we've wasted our time here. Many eastern teachings extol the virtues of a precious human birth, because it's a chance for us to jump ship and reach enlightenment. After all, it's hard to meditate or read scriptures when you're a dung beetle. This life *is* absolutely precious, but that means that the human experience, with all of its vagaries, is equally precious. Each heartbreak, each devastation, each new infatuation allows us to hone our art, making us ever more aware that we're part of some grand drama whose ending we haven't read. We're just characters in a play, actors serving the art of God.

When the matinee is over, we walk out of the theater into the light of day and leave the drama behind. Yes, we'll remember certain moments as great or others as nerve-wracking, but ultimately, we know it was just a trick of stage lights and fog machines. We've done our *dharma*, we gave a performance they'll be talking about for years, whether *devic* or demonic, and now we can enjoy a post-show glass of wine and smoke a well-earned cigarette.

CHAPTER 5

THE DAILY GRIND

W e think playing the role of a yogi means wearing orange robes and running away to the Himalayas to sit in meditation for years. After all, that's the path of the real yogis, the ones who expound upon the eternal *dharma*, telling us married, bill-paying, child-wrangling, job-holding sorts that someday, if we're lucky, we'll be born to a family of Indians or Tibetans who will hand us over to a monastery. American yoga teachers look to the great masters of the past for guidance, and they parrot the words of these saintly swamis and cave-dwelling yogis about the noble path of the earnest seeker who leaves it all behind for the only thing that matters: enlightenment. Your friends, your ailing parents, your children, your jobs – it's all just getting in the way of the Eternal. At the very least, there's an unspoken enshrinement of the monastic life, because we're all literally bowing before the men and women who wear orange; we're spending thousands to join them on retreat or purchase their books; we come away from their talks wanting what they've got. When you're picking up dog shit every day and tripping over a child's plate of spaghetti, it's easy to look longingly at the monk's journey and think, "That's the way to peace."

Some people actually do throw over their Western lives, travel to the east and meditate along the banks of the Ganges before taking holy orders. Some of us go that route because it's our destiny. A greater number of us walk that road, though, because some well-meaning teacher pointed out the way and said, "I don't know. Do what the sages do."

In many ways, they're absolutely right. What else are we to do but follow the people we revere and do what they say down to the letter? Yet we're not here to be anyone other than ourselves. Again, Krishna says that struggling in our own *dharma* – the *dharma* of the householder, perhaps – is far better than succeeding at someone else's. The path of the sage who renounces everything worked for that person, but it doesn't mean it's going to work for you. They had a date with a destiny that led them into caves and alongside rivers. Your destiny could bring you to a house filled with kids and a garage with a mini-van. We look down on the path of the householder, because we're told that it's a treacherous journey, but what if we've got it all wrong? What if the everyday path – the lovers, the kids, the job, the relatives –is the spiritual Olympics where we prove our mettle? The life of the monk could be the icing on a cake made by householders.

⚒

The ol' ball and chain: Veda Vyasa, the great sage born of the fisher girl and the *rishi*, had a son named Suka Deva. The boy left home at a young age to study with a great guru, and he dedicated himself fiercely to his learning. After a decade of study, the now-young man returned home to his delighted father, Vyasa, and the sage said, "It's time you took a wife, my child."

Suka Deva blanched. "How can you ask that of me, father? You, of all people, know that a wife binds a man to this world. A married man only thinks of how to support his wife and children when he should be training his mind solely on God."

Vyasa tried to convince his son about the necessity of finding a wife and fathering children, but Suka Deva again expressed his dismay.

"Like heavy chains dragging a man to the ocean floor, so do a wife and family send a man deep into the ocean of *samsara*, this existence of birth, death and rebirth. I want none of it!"

"Didn't your guru teach you about the four sacred stages of a life?" asked Vyasa. "*Brahmachari, Grihastha, Vanaprastha* and *Sannyasa* – each one a successor to the last. First, we are asked to live a life of celibacy, focusing all our energy on learning, which is an easy thing to do as a child. When we come of age, we marry and fulfill all the roles of a householder. Our children grow and someday have children of their own and only then is it time for us to hand the household over to the younger people and retire to the forest, studying the holy books, doing charitable acts and meditating. Towards the final years, we give up all contact with others, seek solitude and meditate fiercely on the One. My son, even Manu, the progenitor of humanity, said the householder stage is superior to all the others. Follow his words if you don't believe mine!"

Suka Deva stared at his father in disbelief, and silently the young man offered up a prayer to the goddess *Maya*. If She could delude even his august father, then, indeed, She was the greatest power in the world. Suka Deva continued to study and meditate in the forest, skipping the natural progression of life and living as a hermit, yet he was plagued by inner conflict and torment over the path. Nothing was coming quickly enough. He was still trapped in this world of illusion. Noticing this, Vyasa said, "My son, I know you won't listen to me, but go see King Janaka. He rules an entire kingdom, and yet he is a fully enlightened man."

"Not possible," declared Suka Deva.

"Just see him!"

Not one to ignore the wishes of his elders (and if truth be told, he was curious how a man could be both enlightened and a householder), Suka Deva travelled through jungles and over mountain peaks, finally arriving at the rich palace of the great King Janaka. The young holy man was shown to a royal apartment where women were sent to wait on him and fulfill whatever desires he had. They cooked for him, showed him around the gardens and flirted with him, clearly willing to demonstrate their skills in the arts of love, yet he was completely indifferent to their seductions. Seeing that their advances were in vain, they made up the bed for him and departed. He meditated for hours, slept on the floor and then well before dawn, he rose and meditated for three more hours before finally meeting the king.

The great Janaka was delighted at meeting Suka Deva, for Veda Vyasa was the king's own guru. The young man was reserved, though, wary of this householder's supposed exalted spiritual understanding.

"My father says you've reached *moksha*, and you are a *jivanmukta*, a soul liberated while living," said Suka Deva distantly. "Tell me, how is this possible?"

With humble honesty, Janaka replied, "It's actually vital for people to enter the hustle and bustle of the world, finding honor, wisdom and detachment through their interactions with others. It's the best of all ashrams, because here we come face-to-face with what's deep inside our minds." He looked into Suka Deva's penetrating, yet ultimately troubled eyes and said, "Many people want to skip the second stage of life, going straight to renunciation, but such people only bring misery on themselves and confuse avoidance with renunciation."

The young *brahmin* felt as if he'd been slapped; there was a ring of truth to the older man's words. He quickly looked away from the king, dismissing him by saying, "The world is a trap, like a spider's web. Better to get out of the web instead of waiting here to be devoured."

"There are many who think they're ready for the renunciate's life," said Janaka gently, knowing that the young man spoke from pain and not rudeness. "Their senses are withdrawn. There's no interest in the things of this world, so they head out to the forest to commit themselves to God.

"But it's not that easy, my friend. Desires rear their heads, and out there in the woods, there's no opportunity for a man to actually fulfill them – eating good food, having a wife, seeing his children grow. All those meditative hours in the jungle are filled with thoughts of the very things he's trying to escape. You're right, desires are like a web, and they're hard to overcome. Far better to cut your way out of the net slowly than to thrash about and entangle yourself further."

Suka Deva furrowed his brow and gazed down at the floor, trying to parse out the seemingly wise words he was hearing from what he knew of the scriptures. Janaka looked fondly on the young man's struggle, almost as if he was his own son.

"When besieged by these latent desires," said Suka Deva, tightly, feeling as if he was on a raft blowing out to sea against his will, "the hermit can travel to sacred sites and take pilgrimages to cleanse his mind and soul. You can't pick up and tend to your spiritual needs, because a whole kingdom would falter. You're in prison, and I'm free."

"Bondage is in the mind, not the body," Janaka said. "I can do my duty towards this kingdom without being attached to any of it."

"You can't possibly not be attached to all these things!" said Suka Deva, his voice rising in frustration. Two guards entered the room to check on their lord, but he waved them away while Suka Deva continued getting angrier and angrier. "You're the king! With all your money, and your lands, and your harem of women, you're saying you could walk away from all of it in a moment?

When an enemy threatens your kingdom or your wealth or your people, you must feel anger as you sally forth to kill others. When your wives bicker amongst themselves, ruining your few peaceful moments in the quiet of your chambers, you can't concentrate on God. The endless business of running the kingdom takes you out of the temple, not deeper into it!" He was shouting by now, like a young child desperately trying to win an argument with a parent. "I, on the other hand, will be in the forest, with only the deer for company towards whom I have no debt or interest. I'll eat what I find, simple roots and berries. There will be no need to scratch out a life, because I'll be beyond all that. I'll have reached *moksha*, and you'll be stuck in this pit of death, decay and filth for lifetimes on end!"

"We're not as different as you think," said Janaka patiently. "You still have to eat. You still have to find shelter. How much time will you have for meditation when you're digging through the undergrowth for a root or climbing trees to find fruit only to discover that the monkeys have gotten to it first? What about the nights where the tigers are prowling near your camp, waiting for you to turn your back before jumping on you and tearing out your spine with their fangs? Where will all your yogic calm be then?"

Without a word, Suka Deva stalked toward the door, intending to crawl into a cave and forget the idiocy of this king, his stupid father and this entire stinking world.

"You came to me, because your heart is full of doubt, and yet I am seeking no one and nothing," Janaka said in a kingly voice, stopping the young man at the door. "I have no doubts about the wisdom passed to me from my guru, your very father. You are bound because you think you are bound. I am free because I know there is no bondage."

Suka Deva froze. Unwillingly, tears filled his eyes. A heavy burden had suddenly been lifted from his heart, and he was able to take a full breath possibly for the first time in his life. It was all in his head, all the torment, all the obsession with finding *moksha*, the burning desire to flee the world. He had created his own hell.

"Renunciation is a state of being, not an outward display of poverty," he whispered to himself. Suka Deva turned, walked to the king and prostrated himself fully on the floor, where his tears washed the marble beneath the royal saint's feet.

After spending a few more days in Janaka's kingdom, Suka Deva returned to his father, ready for marriage. The young *brahmin*, as handsome as he was intelligent, quickly found a wife and after many years of happiness, fathering children, seeing them take spouses and beholding grandchildren with his own eyes, Suka Deva retired from the world. He journeyed up to Lord Shiva's sacred mountain, Kailash, and there he merged with the infinite reality that is God.

Suka Deva went to Janaka with an agenda, convinced he was right and ready to expose the king as a fraud; after all, Suka Deva had spent several years with his guru where the teachings are supposedly purest. Renounce. Meditate. Transcend. We're always taught to rise above the muck of the world, like that proverbial lotus flower used so often in Eastern symbolism to represent the soul's journey out of the sludge and into the light. Yet if that lotus flower didn't have roots in the dirt, it wouldn't exist.

There is no climb towards the sunlight without a firm foundation in the mud, because we need it, and because, ultimately, there is no difference between sunlight and mud, between God and the world. We're not here to transcend anything. God is beyond this place, yes, but God is also pervasive throughout the world, our lives and ourselves. That Divine force is *both* transcendent and immanent, out there in some pretty heaven and inside the excrement created by the body. So much of what we're taught about yoga – play nice, be fair, eschew judgment, feelings are bad, life is a trap – is handed to us in a neat, pretty package that doesn't measure up to the robust insanity of life. The surface teachings and the truth of yogic belief are seemingly at odds with each other, almost like a love interest playing hard to get. It's as if yoga itself is ferreting out whether or not we're ready for the God-awful truth that it's going to lay at our feet like a precious gem in a pile of shit.

⇒⋅⇐

The wages of sin: There once lived a young *brahmin* man named Gunanidhi, and he was drop-dead gorgeous. He was so beautiful that his guru's wife longed to have him in her bed, and one day, he happily obliged her. They met as often as could be done without raising the master's suspicion, but they both fantasized about a day when they could make love whenever they wanted to, out from under the eye of the guru. Gunanidhi finally poisoned the old man, and the pair told the villagers that he had died of snakebite. No one knew the truth or even suspected it, thinking instead that the handsome disciple cared for the widow out of devotion to his master.

About a month later, the scoundrel's parents came to visit their son and walked in on him and the not-so-grief-stricken widow going at each other like dogs in heat. Gunanidhi's parents cried out in shock, and when he looked up from his lover and saw their horror-stricken faces, Gunanidhi realized he was in deep danger. No one could ever find out what he had done and whom he'd become. Quickly, without thinking further, he grabbed a cooking knife and stabbed them both, dragging their bodies far into the jungle late at night.

Gunanidhi inherited his father's wealth, and he and his mistress began living in high style. One night, during one of his increasingly regular drunken benders out on the town, he began spewing the truth about his widow lover and the demise of his parents. The jig now up, the shocked villagers banished the pair, and Gunanidhi fled to the jungle, leaving the woman to her own fate. He survived by attacking travelers, especially *brahmins*, whom he killed before stealing all their possessions.

After a life of debauchery and cruelty, Gunanidhi died in the very jungle where he'd left his parents' bodies to rot. The dreaded Yamadutas, terrifying servants of the god of death, came to drag the sinner to the worst hells he could ever imagine, but at that exact moment a band of *ganas*, the fantastical servants of Lord Shiva, arrived to stop them and bring Gunanidhi to Shiva's blessed realm.

"There's no way this one has earned that grace," said one of the Yamadutas, disbelievingly. "He seduced his guru's wife before killing him; he murdered his own parents; he slit the throats of countless other innocent holy men and women and stole from them to boot. He's *got* to be punished."

The *ganas* shrugged. "Who are we to go against Lord Shiva's will? Fifteen feet below where he died, down that hill there," pointed the *ganas*, "is a *rudraksha* tree, Shiva's favorite tree, considered blessed by all his *bhaktas*. All his sins have been forgiven. He comes with us."

And, indeed, the *ganas* took Gunanidhi to Shiva, where he became the great Kubera, the god of wealth.

On this path, there is no failure. No matter how terrible you've been in one life or in many, slowly, relentlessly you march towards enlightenment. Even after committing truly awful crimes, eventually you will recognize the supreme truth of your union with God. Gunanidhi was a criminal by any count – murder, betrayal, theft – yet he was rescued from hell and even transformed into a god! All of life boils down to some strange, inexplicable game of chance where time is the only master. Did Gunanidhi, like Lahiri Mahasya, need to fulfill a particular desire or live out a certain karmic circumstance in order to achieve his enlightenment?

Perhaps all the virtue he accumulated from previous lives, which seems ample given his ultimate end, culminated in a death close to that soul-saving *rudraksha* tree. All his good acts constelled to bring him to that place at that precise moment to send him on to the ultimate paradise.

We think we know what's going on in life. We pretend as if we're in control of our own days, when actually we're anything but. You could be dead before putting down this book. People of all ages are dying at a rate of about a hundred per minute. Frailty is the human condition. Death is the human condition. Things ending, going awry, our expectations blown to hell is the human condition. We play along with the farce of a happy, successful life, because it makes living bearable. Facing the demise not just of our bodies, but of our expectations about what life is going to do for us, is an ugly business. It's far nicer to keep calm and carry on – nothing to see here, just step over the bodies – and the yoga business, one of the places that should rub our noses in the stinking decay at our feet, is tragically joining ranks with the rest of the self-deluded soldiers. This life is a one-way ticket, and not only are we not at the helm, we're riding in steerage.

The scriptures of India say that the only way we attain *moksha* is through the grace of God. We can hold one arm over our heads until it withers, as some yogis have done. We can meditate until we don't remember our names anymore. We can follow every single rule laid out by yogis and yogic texts, but in the end, none of that means a thing. A murderer can still become a god.

Indian cosmology lays out four ages that cycle through thousands upon thousands of years. There's a golden age, where everything is perfect, the earth is fruitful, people are beyond virtuous and spend most of their time in spiritual practice. *Dharma* is likened to an animal standing firmly on all four of its legs. When this blessed age comes to a close, covetousness enters the world for the first time and therefore humanity is somewhat tainted, less able to focus on spiritual pursuits, and more interested in accumulating things. In this lesser era, *dharma* has one broken leg, but three out of four ain't bad. Next comes a period when people have started to abandon *dharma*, which now limps along on only two legs. Violence is the order of the day and greed has gained a strong foothold, but still there are those who cling to the old ways and fervently worship the gods. Finally comes the dreaded *kali yuga*, the iron age (not to be confused with the name of the great mother goddess Kali). In this nefarious epoch, people have abandoned themselves to the most lewd and debased behavior, and *dharma* drags itself through the muck with only one crippled leg. Humanity has all but forgotten how to make itself one with the divine, preferring instead an obsessive pursuit of wealth, war, sex and power. Many believe that we are living in the *kali yuga* today, and when it ends, some thousands of years from now, the world will be washed clean and will start anew in the golden age.

India's sacred stories often read like paeans to that faraway exalted era when sages, kings and even the everyday people lived for thousands of years immersed in sacred practices, focused solely on their gods. Despite the lurking shadows of greed and violence that appear in later ages, the characters still cleave to the ways of *dharma*; they follow the holy books and the word of the gurus who ferry them across life's difficult waters to the opposite shore of enlightenment.

Now, however, in our day, the rituals and practices seem like some storybook fantasy that has no relevance to this world, this time, this madness. How are we to navigate the craziness of modern life by following rules from those pristine times?

We don't.

Now is not the time for classical-era strictures and rituals. Times are more dire than that. Some of the sages of the past, figures like the mighty Parasara, pointed out in their purer ages that the teachings are eternal, but the interpretations and executions of them need to change with the times. We can't practice yoga, the art of coming into union with God, in the same way we did when *dharma* stood firmly on four legs, grazing in a field. The creature is caked with filth, bellowing in agony and crawling from one shit pile to another with three mangled limbs dragging behind it. We *must* try other ways.

Why is it that a murderer can become a god? Why does Krishna, in the *Bhagavad Gita*, repeatedly say that *bhakti*, loving devotion to God, trumps techniques of self-inquiry and good works? Why do Jaya and Vijaya achieve an eternal place next to God after becoming ravening creatures of evil? Why does Devi grant liberation to terrible demons who fall in love with Her in their very death throes?

Because, now, in this time, when we're not the kind of people capable of severe *tapas* or endless worship, when the way to peace is so littered with corpses that all we can do is stand and scream hysterically amidst the rot, we can't afford to play small. Leave the practices, the rules, the proscriptions and the pharisaical posturing behind and instead opt for brutal honesty, an unflinching gaze at your own dark materials and a full commitment to life in all of its glory and horror. Step onto the stage ready to howl with grief, laugh with delight, roar with rage, sob with gratitude, quiver with lust and lash out in cruelty. Do it all with total devotion and fierce passion, because these are our rituals now. These are the fires we light, the mantras we chant and the sacrifices we make in honor of the gods.

Sept 23 2016

My Deepest Desires:

- To have integrity & everyone to know
- To be as strong as a man but with a woman's mind
- To be very sexy/sexual and be able to handle it.
- To be really smart and have others accept it/know it.
- to be a leader
- to be excellent @ my crafts
- to be unafraid/courageous in the face of evil, meanness, bigotry
- to express myself with no doubt no fear of reprisal
- to have faith in myself
- To trust myself.
- To be a fixer
- To be a guru

How does it affect the way I live & make decisions?

- To be a badass; cool & calm unflappable

GLOSSARY

These are basic definitions of yogic terms, philosophical concepts and mythological characters used in the book. The meanings and connotations behind India's myths, philosophy and language are downright labyrinthine, and while no short reference can ever capture the nuances of an idea, this is at least a starting point.

Ahimsa – mentioned, perhaps most famously, in Patanjali's *Yoga Sutras* as the virtue of non-harming.

Arjuna – One of the five Pandava brothers. A legendary archer and hero who is the first to hear the *Bhagavad Gita* straight from the mouth of Krishna.

Asuras – Demons. Their name means "without light." The first race created by Brahma.

Bhagavad Gita – One of India's great spiritual texts, it expounds upon truths that are foundational to both Hinduism and yoga.

Bhakti – Often called a form of yoga, *bhakti* is the path of devotional love for a deity. Westerners most famously know it from the singing and dancing Hare Krishna movement, popularized in the late '60s and through the '70s.

Brahma – The creator god. One of the male holy trinity of the Hindu pantheon. (Not to be confused with *brahmin* or *Brahman*. See below.)

Brahmachari – The first of four classic stages of a Hindu life. When a person is a child and adolescent, they devote their time to study, ignoring the other callings of the world (i.e. marriage, making money, etc.). *Brahmacharya* is also a principle in yogic philosophy meaning celibacy or the conservation of energy – mostly through sexual restraint.

Brahman – This is the ultimate (and ultimately unknowable) über-God, who is beyond names, descriptions, forms and attributes. It has no personality, no rules, nothing that the human analytical mind can grasp. All the other gods (e.g. Shiva, Lakshmi, etc.) are masks of Brahman. Brahman is like an ancient Greek actor, playing different roles and therefore wearing different masks every night; we only know the artist through its characters.

Brahmin – One of the four classes in the caste system (the others being *kshatriya* – see below – *vaishya*, the merchant class, and *sudra*, the blue collar workers). *Brahmins* are the priestly class.

Citta vritti – In the *Yoga Sutras*, *citta vritti* are the whirling fluctuations of the mind. According to Patanjali, yoga is the stilling of the spinning mind.

Deva – A certain rank of the gods. The *devas* are often the Vedic gods of wind, fire, death and storms, almost akin to what is more familiar to the Westerner in the Greek gods.

Devi – The Goddess. While there are many goddesses in India, Devi is often portrayed as a composite of them all, the divine feminine that embodies all goddesses everywhere. She is seen as above and beyond the *devas* and, depending on the text, beyond Brahma, Vishnu and Shiva.

Dharma – One's duty or purpose. Also, righteousness.

Durga – The great warrior goddess who rids the world of seemingly unconquerable demons. She and Devi are sometimes interchangeable.

Duryodhana – The cousin of Arjuna and the other Pandava brothers. Duryodhana plunges the kingdom of India into a terrible war because of his jealousy and hatred of the Pandavas.

Gana – A divine devotee of Shiva. Often a fantastical creature (animal heads, multiple arms, etc.) that spends time romping with Shiva wherever he goes and worshipping him.

Grihastha – The second stage of a classical Hindu lifetime. An individual gets married, sets up a home, has children and works to pay the rent.

Jivanmukta/jivamukti – A soul liberated while still living, as opposed to waiting until after death of the body to reach enlightenment. This is not to be confused with Jivamukti Yoga, a popular style of yoga that took its name from the concept.

Kali – The dark-skinned, ferocious mother goddess of India.

Kali yuga – Not related to the goddess Kali (which has a different spelling in Sanskrit), the *kali yuga* is one of the four cosmic ages in the Hindu accounting of time. It's characterized by violence, greed, degradation, misery and spiritual torpor.

Krishna – One of the most famous of Vishnu's ten incarnations, Krishna is central to both the *Mahabharata* and the *Bhagavad Gita*. He is Vishnu come into the world to start a war, wipe out millions, deliver great spiritual teachings and awaken divine love in devotees. (If you grew up Catholic, the Vishnu-Krishna connection is very much like Jesus in the Holy Trinity.)

Kshatriya – One of the Hindu caste classifications, the *kshatriyas* are warriors, knights and political rulers.

Lingam – The erect phallus image often used in worship of Shiva.

Mahabharata – An epic to end all epics, the story follows the travails and triumphs of the five Pandava brothers as they seek to regain their kingdom and establish *dharma* in a world beset by madness.

Maya – Illusion. The term is also used when referring to the world, which is a playground of *maya*. Both illusion and the world itself are synonymous with a goddess of the same name; *maya* and *Maya*, illusion and the goddess of illusion, are one and the same.

Moksha – Liberation from ignorance.

Ojas – Often linked to sexual fluids, ojas is a subtle and/or energetic substance that contributes to one's immunity, energy and, ultimately, wisdom.

Pandavas – The five "good guys" of the *Mahabharata*. Their ancestral lands are stolen by Duryodhana, and they suffer all kinds of trials to get them back, including the great war that wipes out the *kshatriya* race before the onset of the *kali yuga*.

Patanjali – The author of the *Yoga Sutras*.

Prakriti – The world of manifestation and our changing experience in it. Every thing is part of *prakriti*, including our senses, thoughts and emotions.

Rig Veda – The oldest of the four *Vedas*, or foundational scriptures of Hinduism.

Rishi – A seer or great sage.

Sadhana – A spiritual practice.

Sannyasa – The fourth stage in a classical Hindu life. This is where the individual, usually elderly, leaves all human contact behind, goes somewhere isolated and meditates solely upon God, preparing for death.

Sattvic – A particular quality of *prakriti* that is light, clear, peaceful and manifests as positive growth. (The other qualities are *rajas*, sharp and active, and *tamas*, dark and destructive.) *Sattva* relates not only to the gross physical world but one's mental-emotional experience as well.

Shakti – Another name for the goddess. She is pure, untrammeled power and energy. All the male gods have "their" Shakti, their feminine half that is that god's ability to act in the way relative to that god (e.g. Shiva cannot be the destroyer without his Shakti, he would be unable to do anything – a great visual representation of this is in images of Kali standing over a prone Shiva who is often pictured as inert).

Shiva – One of the Hindu male trinity, Shiva is frequently called the destroyer, although that is too simplistic a designation. Destruction both destroys and creates, and Shiva is the same. He is a yogi *par excellence*, meditating in the Himalayas for eons, and he's also a wild hash-smoking dancer who hangs out with goblins and ghosts. A fully integrated guy.

Sudarshana chakra – One of Vishnu's famous weapons that is often described as a wheel having a varying number of sharp spokes, almost like a cosmic rotary saw.

Tapas, tapasva – Heat caused by friction, not just in the obvious striking of a match, but more of the inner heat caused by friction through overpowering our own will. In yoga, this takes the form of austerities (e.g. holding one's arm overhead for years). A *tapasva* is someone who has performed these acts successfully and gained enormous power as a result.

Vanaprastha – The third stage of a classical Hindu life takes place after one no longer needs to fulfill their householder roles. The children are grown. One's career is wrapping up. At this point, the individual retires to the forest, doing acts of charity and becoming more involved with spirituality.

Vishnu – Part of the Hindu male trinity, Vishnu is labeled "the pre-server." Whenever *dharma* is threatened in the world, he incarnates to set things right. There are ten of his avatars; the last one is still waiting in the wings.

Yamaduta – A servant of Yama, the god of death. The Yamadutas often go to retrieve a soul at the time of a person's demise.

Yoga Sutras – Of all the texts cited by Western yoga teachers and students, Patanjali's *Yoga Sutras* seems to get pride of place. It's a collection of short and rich aphorisms about the practice of yoga, although it has almost nothing to do with *asana* but focuses, instead, on the capacity for yoga/union in one's own consciousness.

ACKNOWLEDGMENTS

To all the incredible yoga practitioners I've met – you're the real teachers. I'm constantly inspired by and in awe of the way you walk the paths of yoga.

To Brendan, thanks for five years of reminding me what my chart says about writing. I'm slow, but eventually I listened. Also for the countless book recommendations, classes and other signposts of wisdom. (For more information on Brendan Feeley, a man I can't recommend highly enough for Hindu astrology or Ayurveda, visit bpfeeley.com.)

To Cat, thank you for a gorgeous cover design and making an actual book.

Anne, your advice in the process of self-publishing was beyond helpful.

Thank you to the readers who provided incredible feedback– Subha for your invaluable input on the Indian myths, Stephenie for your thoughtful words about consistency and Corrine for making me go the distance.

To the various translators and storytellers of the Hindu canon to whom I turned for my own study and then retellings in this book (notably Ramesh Menon), thank you for opening up this intoxicating world of Hindu myth to English speakers. Also a note of clarification for readers – all the stories in this book are gleaned from source materials (the *Shiva Purana,* the *Srimad Devi Bhagavatam,* the *Mahabharata,* etc.), but also told from the perspective of my own imagination.

To a man I never knew personally but who has guided my thoughts and way of viewing the world since I was 16: Joseph Campbell, I offer my deep gratitude (and full credit for the fantastic line "Former Indras all").

To my mother and stepfather, René and Chuck, your proofreading abilities come to the rescue for yet another writer. Thank you for not only tending to the letter, but also the spirit. (And for being amazing parents, of course.)

Finally, to Jordan for his stalwart ability to wrangle all my neuroses while still keeping it sexy, for endless discussions about this point or that point, for managing to actually look engaged while I waffled on about some new myth and for reminding me to put the book down and eat something. I love you.

Made in the USA
Middletown, DE
11 October 2015